Suicide in Prisons

Prisoners' Lives Matter

Graham J Towl and David A Crighton

Foreword Lord Toby Harris

≫ WATERSIDE PRESS

Suicide in Prisons: Prisoner's Lives Matter
Graham J Towl and David A Crighton

ISBN 978-1-909976-44-3 (Paperback)
ISBN 978-1-910979-29-7 (Epub E-book)
ISBN 978-1-910979-30-3 (Adobe E-book)

Cover design © 2017 Waterside Press by www.gibgob.com

Printed by Lightning Source.

Main UK distributor Gardners Books, 1 Whittle Drive, Eastbourne, East Sussex, BN23 6QH. Tel: +44 (0)1323 521777; sales@gardners.com; www.gardners.com

North American distribution Ingram Book Company, One Ingram Blvd, La Vergne, TN 37086, USA. Tel: (+1) 615 793 5000; inquiry@ingramcontent.com

Cataloguing-In-Publication Data A catalogue record for this book can be obtained from the British Library.

e-book *Suicide in Prisons: Prisoner's Lives Matter* is available as an ebook and also to subscribers of Ebrary, Ebsco, Myilibrary and Dawsonera.

Published 2017 by
Waterside Press Ltd
Sherfield Gables
Sherfield on Loddon, Hook
Hampshire RG27 0JG.

Telephone +44(0)1256 882250
Online catalogue WatersidePress.co.uk
Email enquiries@watersidepress.co.uk

Table of Contents

Acknowledgments

We would like to acknowledge with grateful thanks Dr Camila Caiado for her help with formatting the chapters.

Our thanks also go to to those experts in various areas of the field of prisoner suicide who read the manuscript ahead of publication and whose individual comments appear before the start of the book.

About the authors

Professor David A Crighton MA MSc PhD FBPsS FAcSS Chartered Psychologist, HCPC Registered Psychologist.

David Crighton is a Consultant Psychologist and Honorary Professor of Psychology at Durham University. He is also a Visiting Professor at Roehampton University, London and a number of other universities. He has longstanding research and practice interests in suicide within a range of forensic settings and has published extensively in this area. He has previously been a member of the World Health Organization Working Group on Suicide in Prisons and also contributed to the Royal College of Psychiatrists' Working Group on Violence in Secure Settings. He has previous experience of working in National Health Service forensic, mental health and forensic learning disability services and has been employed as a Consultant Clinical Psychologist in the NHS, as Regional Psychologist for Prisons and Probation in Kent, Surrey and Sussex, London, and as Deputy Head of Psychology for Prisons and Probation and Deputy Chief Psychologist in the United Kingdom's Ministry of Justice.

Professor Graham J Towl RMN, BA, MSc, MBA, DSc, FRSA, FBPsS, FRSM, FAcSS, Chartered Psychologist, HCPC Registered.

Graham Towl is Professor of Forensic Psychology at Durham University and Visiting Clinical Professor at Newcastle University. Uniquely he is the recipient of both the British Psychological Society's Award for Distinguished Contributions to Professional Psychology and for Distinguished Contributions to Forensic Academic Knowledge. He was peer nominated as the most influential forensic psychologist in the United Kingdom. His interest in prison suicide has spanned nearly 30 years with experience in practice, policy and research. He co-edited the standard British Psychological Society handbook on *Suicide in Prisons* in 2000 (with Martin McHugh and Louisa Snow). Along with David Crighton he was the first person in the UK to highlight the data on ethnicity when considering prisoner suicides. In the 1990s, he was a practitioner in prisons and chaired the National Research Forum of the Suicide Awareness Support Unit (SASU) within HM Prison Service. In 2000 he was appointed as Head of Psychological Services in Prisons and Probation for England and Wales. He remains an advocate of, evidence informed policy and practice implemented with kindness and a compassionately based professionalism. His publications include *Preventing Self-injury and Suicide in Women's Prisons* (with Tammi Walker) (Waterside Press, 2016).

The author of the Foreword

Lord Toby Harris was Chair of the Independent Advisory Panel on Deaths in Custody from 2009 to 2015. In February 2014, he was asked by the Minister for Prisons to lead the review into self-inflicted deaths in National Offender Management Service (NOMS) custody. This was completed in April 2015, published in July 2015, and made recommendations to reduce the risk of such deaths.

Reviews

'A superb publication and coming at exactly the right time. This book cuts through the rhetoric with a forensic analysis of the problems coupled with practical, low cost and rapidly achievable recommendations. It makes for uncomfortable but essential reading.'

John Podmore, International Prisons Consultant and former Prison Governor.

'Rarely has a book been more timely or pertinent than this one ... Towl and Crichton offer a thorough, wide-ranging and nuanced account of suicides in prison which contextualises, describes and analyses 36 years of data. It offers both extensive detail and concise introductory and concluding chapters ... combining encyclopedic coverage of theory and data with a call to arms.'

Philippa Tomczak, PhD Criminology Research Fellow, School of Law, University of Sheffield and Leverhulme Trust Early Career Research Fellow.

'This timely addition to the debate about self-inflicted deaths in prison places the issue firmly in the context of theoretical perspectives, recent research and expert commentaries. Towl and Crichton identify current difficulties, including common misconceptions, and suggests a new approaches to reduce suicides in prison. A book ... that does not pull it punches!'

Carol Robinson, Doctoral Researcher, University of York.

'*Suicide in Prisons: Prisoners' Lives Matter* is an important book about a subject that receives too little attention. Drawing on 36 years of data, it argues that prisoners' lives matter and current policies regarding incarceration need to be revised in light of the growing number of prison suicides. It is essential reading for anyone who works within a prison system, and hopefully will lead to changes.'

John Bateson, San Francisco, author, former suicide prevention counsellor.

'This book is a must for anyone undertaking research and policy work in this area. It provides a great overview of the historical, political, and social context—exploring why people in prison are at increased risk of taking their own lives. It reminds us that prisoners are not a representative cross-section of society, and that as researchers we have a responsibility to put any work in this context. Addressing the fact that the prison population is made up of the most disadvantaged in our society, the authors draw links between factors of inequality, inequity and suicide, alongside the nuances of the prison system. They critically explore what research has taught us thus far, and make thought-provoking recommendations about future work to influence policy and practice. It has the potential for great impact, and can be the starting point for changing opinions, policies, systems and lives for the better.'

Elizabeth Scowcroft, BSc, MSc, Nottingham Trent University and The Samaritans.

'This book makes harrowing reading. It doesn't take much to join the dots and make the link between the massive cuts to prison budgets and the horrendous increase in suicide and self-harm. Yet the media venom towards people who are locked up continues which dictates Government policy. But how can we punish people who are already punishing and in some cases killing themselves? When will someone at the highest level of Government be held accountable for the deaths of people's loved ones?'

Mark Johnson, User Voice.

'The book provides a clear and concise summary of the existing studies on suicide in prisons, as well as original research and analysis. The broad coverage of academic research, policy and organizational issues is particularly valuable for students interested in this important topic.'

Dominic Aitken, PhD Student, Oxford University

Foreword

Lord Toby Harris

Three years ago, I was asked by the Minister for Prisons to lead a review into the self-inflicted deaths of young people aged 18 to 24 in prisons or young offender institutions. My panel included Graham Towl, one of the authors of this book, and many of the statistics here were drawn on during the review process.

The review[1] reported in the summer of 2015 and, whilst some of its key recommendations were initially rejected by the Ministry of Justice, the recent White Paper[2] clearly draws on many of my review's ideas.

It looked in detail at the cases of 83 young adults who suffered self-inflicted deaths from April 2007 (the point at which the Assessment, Care in Custody, and Teamwork process was rolled out) until the end of 2013. In addition, we looked at the deaths of the four under-18s who died during the same period.

Our conclusions focussed necessarily on the age group of those cases we had examined, but many of our recommendations were applicable to prisoners of all ages.

It is worth remembering that all of the deaths looked at in the review — or in this book — represent individual tragedies. Whatever the events that led to those who died ending up in custody, the people concerned were also someone's son or daughter, sister or brother, partner or parent.

The review looked at an enormous body of evidence and indeed it was probably the most comprehensive independent consideration of penal policy in this country for the last 20 or 30 years.

---

1. The Harris Review (2015) Changing Prisons, Saving Lives, *Report of the Independent Review into Self inflicted Deaths in Custody of 18–24-year-olds*, July, OCL, London.
2. Ministry of Justice (2016) *Prison Safety and Reform*, Cm 9350, Ministry of Justice, London.

Some clear messages emerged. Each of the deaths examined represents a failure by the State to protect the people concerned. And that failure is all the greater because the same criticisms occur time and time again. Lessons have not been learned and not enough has been done to bring about change. It remains to be seen whether the White Paper and the Prisons and Courts Bill now before Parliament will deliver the transformation needed.

The Government has adopted the review's recommendation that there should be a clear statement — now to be enshrined in statute — about the purpose of prison and that rehabilitation should be at its core. It is important that this statement acknowledges that all persons who are deprived of their liberty — and this is the sentence of the court — should be treated with respect for their human rights.

The cohort of young adults whose cases we considered had all to a greater or lesser extent been vulnerable. Most had had chaotic lives and complex histories, some had been subjected to child abuse or exposed to violence, and many had been in foster or residential care. Their problems had often been further compounded by mental health issues.

And despite the stereotype found in some newspapers, prisons and YOIs are grim environments that are bleak and demoralising to the spirit. This makes the experience of being in prison particularly damaging to those who are already vulnerable or whose minds are still developing. Moreover, this is exacerbated where regimes are impoverished and restricted as a result of staff shortages and budget cuts. Our analysis of the 87 deaths reviewed convinced us that many of the vulnerable young adults concerned were going through a period of particular distress that might have passed if they had not been spending so much time inside their cell with nothing to do other than to stare at potential ligature attachment points.

It was apparent in the review that operational staffing levels were not adequate. Since then the Government has announced additional staff, but even when these officers are recruited (if indeed current recruitment problems can be overcome) staff numbers will still not have reached the levels that existed only six or seven years ago.

Without adequate staffing it is difficult to see how the objectives set out for rehabilitation can be met. At present, prisoners are not sufficiently engaged in purposeful activity and time is not spent in a constructive and valuable way. Current restricted regimes do not even allow for the delivery of planned core day activities and during the review we came across frequent examples of medical and mental health appointments being missed because there were not sufficient staff to escort prisoners.

Achieving the rehabilitation objective will require a lot more. Leadership will be critical in this—something that Ministers now say that they accept—and this must be focussed on delivering real cultural change in prisons and YOIs that prioritises ensuring that prisoners are rehabilitated, valued and nurtured towards safer and more productive lives.

This will also require a workforce in prisons that is trained and developed to a higher professional standard than at present and staff will need to be motivated, knowledgeable and compassionate.

The review recommended that responsibility for health, education, social care, safety, and rehabilitation should be taken on by a new category of prison officer. The review called this person a Custody and Rehabilitation Officer and they would be specialist and suitably trained professionals with a small enough caseload so that enough time would be given to each prisoner both to understand their needs and to deliver the services needed to address them. This appears to be mirrored in the idea of the 'dedicated officer' contained in the Prisons White Paper. It remains to be seen whether this intent is maintained as the proposals are rolled out and implemented.

Of course, a reduction in the overall prisoner population would make it easier for prisons to provide an environment that meets appropriate standards of decency, safety and respect. Whilst society would expect most of those currently in prison to have received a custodial sentence, it is apparent that much more needs to be done to support people and divert them away from the conduct that led them into prison long before they were ever in contact with the criminal justice system.

In the 87 cases examined in the review, many of the young people's problems and vulnerabilities, including mental health issues, had been evident from an early age. The question has to be asked what went wrong and why did so many of them end up in custody. The appropriate interventions much earlier in prisoners' lives might well mean that far fewer ended up offending and that far fewer would have ended up in prison.

Prisons are hugely expensive and yet the benefits of this spend, as prisons are presently constituted, are questionable with a relatively low impact on crime and with rates of re-offending that are particularly high among young adults. Reinvestment and redirection of resources into early intervention are likely to deliver better outcomes for the individuals concerned, as well as a smaller and more manageable prison population.

These are policy choices that will require bold and brave Ministers prepared to engage in long-term investment the benefits of which may well not be seen until long after they have left office. I hope this book will help convince them to be bold and brave.

Lord Toby Harris
March 2017

CHAPTER 1

Setting the Scene

Introduction

This book is about suicide in prisons. The approach taken includes a consideration of theoretical perspectives and also a broader consideration of suicide in society. The latter parts of the book draw together research on prisoner suicide. New empirical research into prisoner suicide is also outlined with the largest UK study of its kind. One pervasive theme in the book is how we may most effectively learn from what we know about prisoner suicide and how this may inform prevention.

The brutal reality is that there is generally very little public interest in suicide in prisons. This is despite the extensive recent media coverage of violence in prisons. And this can be selective reporting. For example, staff on prisoner violence is rarely reported in the media, nor is such data routinely provided. The political discourse tends to focus upon 'hard working staff' doing a difficult job, and, of course, there is much truth to this, but it is very far from the whole picture. Prison Service staff are by no means alone as public servants in being subject to violence. There appear to be more incidents of assaults on nurses than prison officers yet the media coverage portrays prisons (rather than hospitals) as dangerous places. And there are dangers. But rarely is this put into a broader perspective of those working with prisoners or patients who may have various vulnerabilities by the fundamental nature of such relationships. Ill patients are highly dependent upon healthcare staff and similarly prisoners are highly dependent upon prison staff to ensure that even their basic needs are met. Such vulnerabilities can beget tensions.

Although women in prisons are over 12 times more likely to complete suicide than in the community and for men around six times more likely, overall rates of deaths in custody are lower than in the community using (crude) standardised mortality rates (IAP, 2017). And it is this complex environment of reduced risks of death overall, but increased levels of risk of self-inflicted deaths for those in prisons compared with the community that provides a backdrop to debates around prisoner suicide. Disturbances or protests, also inform such debates around prisoner and staff safety more generally in prisons. Although statistics that support the notion of prisons in any way being 'safer' in any sense are rarely reported, it simply does not fit with the popular narrative around prisons. Just as the figure claiming over 12 times greater risk for women comes with (statistical) health warnings so does data on crude standardised mortality rates. The rates of prisoner suicide dropped marginally between 2014 and 2015 although curiously, perhaps because it does not fit with a 'crisis' narrative, this does not appear to have been widely reported as such. Nonetheless the overall pattern since records have been kept in 1979 has been one of an upwards trajectory (see *Chapter 9* of this volume).

Human rights

It is a human rights perspective that is taken as our starting point in this book. This is not to deny that those imprisoned are often there because of their acts of human wrongs. There is a duty to preserve and protect the lives of those kept within state custody independently of what crimes they have committed. It is recognised that many in the field would take such rights as axiomatic but it may be helpful to be explicit about such matters for two reasons. First, in terms of values and beliefs, by making these explicit at the beginning of this book any resultant biases may be more readily salient for readers. Second, it is important to be explicit about such values and beliefs because so often such matters are left at the level of the implicit, which in practice may contribute to a vacuum of explicit values. This is arguably especially important in Criminal Justice settings such as prisons, where the ideologies and underpinning values of the institutions of Criminal Justice and Health may be in tension, and at times significant tension. From a human rights perspective although the courts are charged with the enactment of our laws, those delivering such judgements tend to come from particular social groups and are visibly male and white with backgrounds overrepresented in public schools. Thus, the idea of a truly independent court system may be, sometimes viewed as arguably limited, in that it disproportionately may be seen as representing the perspectives of the socially privileged in our communities. In this sense judges and prisoners share a commonality in that neither are representative samples from the community and this may well have consequences for all. Perhaps if judges were more representative there would be a greater awareness of the social context of crime, which may serve to decrease the increasingly marked propensity of the courts to imprison and to imprison for increasingly long periods in recent years. If we were to reduce the prisoner population we would predict a reduction in prisoner suicides. The courts clearly have a role to play in this, not just the Prison Service. Nonetheless the courts can only act within the law set by successive governments, so government clearly has a clear leadership role in this challenging area. And more general public opinion may impact upon both government and court decisions.

So, with imprisonment at about twice the levels of the early-1990s it is clear that there has been stiffer sentencing. Successive government administrations have been involved in a political dialogue around who can 'talk tougher' on crime and punishment. As indicated above, one key way of reducing prisoner suicide would be to reduce the numbers imprisoned. However, we recognise that any significant rational reduction of prisoner numbers would be predicted, on the data, to result in an increase in the rates of prisoner suicide. But there would be highly likely to be a decrease in the overall numbers of cases of suicide. Oftentimes rates and frequencies are conflated in some of the discussions and debates around prisoner suicide. So, for example, older prisoners are at an inflated risk of suicide compared with younger prisoners. However, there are many more young prisoners who complete suicide. But any such overall decrease in numbers would most probably result in increased proportions of those imprisoned being from categories of offence types statistically associated with over representations in the prisoner suicide figures such as violent offenders and those who commit arson and criminal damage.

Fresh perspectives

The previous core textbook exclusively on this area, *Suicide in Prisons* (Towl, Snow and McHugh, 2000) distinctively drew together work on research, policy and practice. Although many of the research findings today largely replicate what was known at the turn of the century when that handbook was written there have been some developments in the research and a number of policy changes too along with some shifts in practice. And we have seen above that there have been significant increases in the numbers of people imprisoned. Less well known is the success of the prison service in reducing the percentage of those who complete suicide in the early stages of their imprisonment. That said, the early period of imprisonment still represents, on average, a period of markedly inflated risk of suicide. The make up of the prisoner population has changed too, with for example, proportionately more imprisoned (convicted) sex offenders than ever before in the UK. This is relevant when looking at suicide in view of the strong evidence of an overrepresentation of violent offenders, in relation to the risks of suicide (see *Chapter 9* of this volume).

One of the distinctive features of this new book is that we incorporate some of the findings of the largest research study to date either historically or internationally, reviewing the data from 1978 when records began for prisons in England and Wales to 2014. Some of this data was used to inform a government commissioned review of self-inflicted deaths of prisoners, aged 18–24 (Harris Review, 2015). Some of the specific findings were also shared with the House of Commons Justice Committee on prison safety through a letter from the then chair of the Independent Advisory Panel on Deaths in Custody, Kate Lampard. Unfortunately, the committee appeared somewhat unconvinced of the evidence mentioned, in particular the reference to the Prison Service success in reducing the percentage of those completing suicide early during their imprisonment.

Some of the original research findings, included in this text have, in view of the pressing nature of the subject matter, started to be shared more widely at conferences in the UK and beyond and have been widely positively received in recognition of both the methodological rigour and prisoner suicide population size (N = 2039). Much of the data has been published solely as descriptive data through the Ministry of Justice. For the first time, though, is an analysis and commentary upon the new data drawing from the records of cases from 1978 through to 2014 as indicated above. We will be including further commentary on the data. Some of the ideas are also the product of exchanges of views at international conferences in Krakow, Vienna and London where some of the ideas and data have been shared with colleagues to stimulate discussion, debate and ultimately a better understanding of prisoner suicide.

We are also keen to look at ways of prison leaders freeing up resources to ensure an improved focus upon saving lives in prisons. Staff recruitment and retention has been an area of challenge manifest in recent years in several arenas. The costs of recruitment, training and lower retention levels are inherently costly due to the expense associated with inducting new staff and the time-lag whilst they are learning. And more staff are needed to focus upon rehabilitation rather than primarily upon security (important though that clearly is). Where there have been rehabilitation-based interventions, some have continued despite growing evidence which calls into question their ineffectiveness. For example, sex offender treatment group work in prisons. Such programmes continue to run yet the evidence in support of their efficacy does not appear to be supported by evaluation data (Crighton and Towl, 2005; Towl and Crighton, 2016) Of course, in public services political expediency may trump empirical evidence. But there are more specific, purportedly, suicide prevention-based areas of work that need stopping if resources are to be freed up to save lives. For example, investments in screening tools, putting prisoners into two categories; suicidal and non-suicidal, is conceptually incoherent. One of the problems with the concept of screening tools which are sometimes used to 'predict' the suicidal and the non-suicidal is that they are implemented as a snapshot assessment at a point in time yet we know that mood states fluctuate sometimes significantly. So, even if an individual did not feel suicidal at one point in time that will not be predictive of them not necessarily feeling suicidal at another point in time, sometimes soon afterwards (yet they may have been allocated to a 'non-suicidal' category by then). A second, and substantive conceptual problem with such screening tools may be referred to as the base rate problem where, for example, there are many prisoners who share the characteristics linked to an inflated risk of suicide e.g. unemployment so it is not possible to reliably use such factors to predict suicide. There are essentially four possible outcomes with such screening tools. First, the accurate prediction of suicide, second the inaccurate prediction of suicide, third the accurate prediction of not completing suicide and fourthly the inaccurate prediction of not completing suicide. The majority of prisoner suicides fall into this latter category although as indicated later in this book, there are some indications of gender differences with such assessments.

The current position of suicide prevention training not being mandatory against a backdrop of increased rates of suicide and widespread concerns about staff and prisoner safety is difficult to defend. When referring to prison staff the term is not simply synonymous with prisons officers. Those providing services in prisons, for example, teachers, catering and workshop staff all would benefit from such training. Sometimes workshop staff or teachers may spend more time with individual prisoners than prison officers and the nature of the relationships in such roles may serve to better facilitate the disclosure of feelings by prisoners. There are parallels with the danger of psychologists employed directly by the Prison Service undertaking chiefly risk assessments focused on the risk of reconviction, sometimes not being viewed as individuals to disclose suicidal feelings too (Towl and Walker, 2016). Indeed, although there are some very legitimate concerns frequently expressed (and these seem entirely legitimate concerns) about the marketisation of Criminal Justice services there have been some surprising but positive opportunities for improving services. Some prisoners may be more willing to disclose feelings, especially perhaps with a matter as sensitive as suicidal feelings, to those not directly employed by the Prison Service. Mandatory suicide prevention training could be built into contracts for outsourced educational and rehabilitation work with the charitable sector. But suicide prevention training is essential as part of the initial training of prison officers and there remains a need to train existing prison officer staff too. Health and social care staff need training too. There remain several myths around suicide in prisons and psychiatrists and psychologists can often promulgate such myths too. We will be exploring and examining common misconceptions about prisoner suicide later in the book. Two of such myths are that remand prisoners are at a greater risk of suicide than sentenced prisoners and that younger prisoners are at a higher risk of suicide than older prisoners. Both are inaccurate beliefs in terms of the data on factors associated with differential rates of suicide amongst prisoners.

But what we will also be covering in this book is the research in terms of both policy and practice implications. This is important because, although some lessons have clearly been learnt in the field from the research it is clear that there is still much that could be done simply in terms of applying the understanding we have more effectively to improved policies and (clinical) practices. Indeed, one central argument throughout this book is that there is a need to address and implement the applications and learning from existing research before considering investing in further research. Advocating no further research is counter intuitive for probably most academic colleagues, but it seems that if we do not take stock and demonstrate learning from the literature with some practical policy and practice changes then, if reducing prisoner suicides is our aim, we will not achieve that goal with research alone. The further needs or interests of the research community need to be considered only after the research has been both thoroughly understood and applied with the impact of reducing preventable deaths by suicide on prisons.

It has become fashionable within health and social care and beyond to use the language of Evidence Based Practice (EBP). It is perhaps noteworthy that bodies such as the Health and Care Professions Council (HCPC) the statutory regulator of 16 health and social care professions has dispensed with the term in their literature preferring instead to use the term, Evidence Informed Practice (EIP). The reason for this change was that it had become increasingly clear that the term EBP has been seen to conceptualise evidence as something that we do or do not have, in support of a particular intervention. Viewing evidence as such a categorical variable seems add odds with what is known about the quality and appropriateness of different methods of evidence acquisition. In other words, there are numerous ways of acquiring evidence. All such methods will have strengths and weaknesses. Traditionally within criminology and health there have been debates about the merits and demerits of what has been framed as a debate between those who advocate mainly quantitative approaches to the evidence gathering process and those who advocate more qualitative based approaches. Both have their place and both may potentially elicit high (or low) quality evidence to inform our understanding of suicide in prisons. In this book, we draw from both and use the term evidence informed practice in recognition of the fact that there are different levels and types of evidence with various strengths and weaknesses. And we do wish to be informed by the evidence. This feeds into a wider debate certainly within the psychological literature, for example, when looking at assessments of the likelihood of a prisoner getting reconvicted or not. Some believe that this is in essence simply a statistical matter whereas others believe that human judgement is important in making decisions that are informed by the evidence. But others argue that such clinical decision making just brings unevidenced potentially confounding factors to the decision making. Actuarially based tools can never take the place of skilled and informed clinicians. The argument is in part about the format of much data, for example, in relation to suicidal prisoners. Much of what we know about those factors linked to a higher risk of suicide amongst prisoners has been gleaned, by definition, from group data. Many of the assertions made, and they are assertions made in terms of the evidence that we will cover in this book, are simply based on averages for a particular group based upon a (usually predetermined) variable. So, for example, we may know that statistically if a prisoner is sentenced for a violent offence then, on average, they will have a higher risk of suicide than a prisoner who is not held for a violent offence. However, the skilled clinician needs to appropriately weight such evidence in relation to any other evidence that they may have. For example, the prisoner may have a great deal of social support and have been at the prison where the assessment is taking place for some time, both would, most probably, be protective features. But it is also an important ethical issue which needs consideration and centres around accountability needing, by definition, to be with a person.

For conceptual convenience in clinical practice we routinely distinguish between 'assessment' and 'treatment' but in practice these are overlapping categories in any clinical formulation. This is because a competent clinician will work in a fashion whereby the way in which any assessment is conducted will be mindful of the need to build rapport and demonstrate respect for the prisoner, which, in turn would be reflected in any such 'treatment'. The importance of the overlapping nature of these categories of the activities of professionals when working with suicidal prisoners cannot be overemphasised. But it is not only professionals who can be of assistance in reducing the risk of suicide in prisons. Schemes such as the Samaritan based Listener schemes can all be potentially helpful but need to be well run with those acting as peer listeners being given appropriate support themselves. There was some resistance to the introduction of peer listening services for prisoners in the 1990s. And this may reflect a broader tension between the needs of the individual prisoner and the (perceived) needs of the public as if they are mutually exclusive categories. If we are to rehabilitate prisoners, compassion and kindness may have more of a role especially with any rapport building process than a stark clinical focus on what has become called a 'targeting' of so called 'criminogenic factors' where the term 'responsivity' seems preferred to every day terms such as 'rapport'. A focus upon the managerial administration of a process to reduce suicides rather than a focus perhaps upon working with prisoners who are feeling suicidal may well be problematic. Earlier we mentioned the problems of psychologists being involved in enacting a function providing reports on the risk of reoffending and how this may reduce the chances of the disclosure of suicidal feelings and thoughts. The two do not have to be mutually exclusive but a high level of skill can be needed to be both viewed as on the one hand a state official working in the interests of the state whilst also retaining clear compassion at an everyday human level. Such challenging issues can be addressed in the training of health and social care professionals and indeed in the training of prison officers too. As we shall see in the chapter on some of the very latest research it appears that prisons are uniquely more toxic for women than they are for men, with young women being at particularly high levels of risk of suicide compared with the rates in the community for young women. The recently announced plans for the recruitment of 2,500 prison officers is to be welcomed. Additionally, there is a compelling case for the recruitment of staff chiefly concerned with rehabilitation. For example, Allied Health Professionals are perhaps an underused multifaceted group of staff who could be of potentially significant help in contributing to suicide prevention. This is not to suggest that prison officers cannot have a role in rehabilitation work too, they clearly can have.

This book is intended as a resource for all those concerned with reducing prisoner suicides. It builds upon previous research, policy and practice work and has one ultimate aim — contributing to reducing prisoner suicides. We hope that you find what you need to contribute to the reduction of prisoner suicide so that there is not the continued preventable loss of life by suicide in our prisons.

CHAPTER 2

Theoretical Perspectives on Suicide

Introduction

It is difficult to adequately understand the view of suicide in the United Kingdom (and indeed in Europe and North America) without considering the dominant Judeo-Christian tradition (Battin, 1996). This provides the foundation for much of the social and legal thinking in this area for centuries. In its early stages, the Christian Church had little to say on the issue of self-inflicted deaths. It later developed a philosophy that strongly opposed such deaths, arguably more so than many other religious traditions.

More recently, theological approaches have been displaced as the dominant basis for understanding suicide. They were gradually replaced by rationalist approaches as typified by medical, psychological and sociological accounts that seek to use scientific approaches to understanding suicide.

A principle of the 'sanctity of life' came to pervade much Christian thinking and in turn this derived in part from Jewish tradition (Battin, 1996). The *Bible* though does not forbid self-inflicted death and those passages generally cited as prohibitions require interpretation.

For example, drawing on the sixth commandment that 'Though shalt not kill', as prohibiting suicide. The early Christian Church had drawn heavily on Plato's views on suicide, but did not appear to have a unified position on the moral status of suicide. This changed through the middle ages and, based largely on the views of St Augustine and later Thomas Aquinas became increasingly hostile to and condemning of suicide.

In Augustine's philosophy, a distinction is made between private killing and killing directed by a divinely constituted authority. This suggested that suicide was not wrong where it was commanded by God. Under such conditions, Augustine suggested obedience is required. Where it was not commanded in this manner it was a sin against God.

This logic came to be increasingly challenged by Enlightenment philosophers. Perhaps the most successful critique was given by John Donne, the 17th-Century moral philosopher. Donne emphasised the central role of individual conscience in determining actions. He saw this as the means of knowing Divine will, rather than the direct commands suggested by Augustine.

English common law drew heavily on such traditions and came to see suicide as a violation of natural law. This remains the philosophical basis for much of the legal approach to suicide in the UK.

More modern conceptions of suicide have adopted scientific approaches to the study of the area and have displaced notions such as Divine commands. They have though generally adopted the view that suicide contravenes normal biological and psychological functioning. As such it is an unnatural or pathological state for any living being.

Post Enlightenment thinking and research on suicide has largely depended on deterministic models. These have seen suicide as resulting from factors outside a person's control. In turn this suggested value in identifying what these factors might be and how they might lead to self-inflicted deaths. Linked to this the notion of developing ways to prevent or ameliorate such factors became important.

Rationalist approaches to suicide

Theological approaches to suicide have increasingly been displaced by more 'scientific' approaches. These initially stressed the role of careful observation and rational explanation, adopting the simplest viable account. The use of experimentation is also central to this approach and in relation to a range of behaviours it has displaced the use of supernatural explanations. Philosophically the approach drew heavily on 'determinism'. The traditional version of this saw suicides as being due to factors beyond individual control. Suicide therefore could not be a rational or autonomous act. In turn this provides the basis for interventions attempting to prevent suicides (Amchin, Wettstein and Roth, 1995).

These models of suicide can be described in terms of three broad types. The first of these might reasonably be termed the 'medical model'. Here suicide is viewed as largely the product of mental disorder or illness. The second approach might be termed a 'psychological model' and seeks to explain suicide in terms of normal patterns of thinking and behaviour. The third broad group of approaches is largely determinist, seeing suicide as the result of social forces such as poverty, unemployment and other forces largely beyond the person's control (Durkheim, 1952). It is worth stressing at the outset that these broad theoretical approaches are not always mutually exclusive. Indeed, the most powerful explanatory models are likely to involve the use of overlapping models.

Medical models of suicide

Medical approaches to suicide largely displaced previous theological models. Suicide is viewed as the product of illness. Those who took their own lives were viewed as sick rather than sinful, in need of treatment rather than criticism. In common with earlier views though, suicide was viewed as in contravention of natural laws, in this case biological laws. This view of suicide is well-established and considered by many to be an orthodoxy (Fairburn, 1995).

Currently advocates of this approach normally see those who kill themselves as suffering from some form of mental disorder. The medical role is therefore to intervene to attempt to treat and cure the underlying disorder (Fairburn, 1995). The suicidal person here is viewed as not fully competent to make decisions about their welfare. This is important because if the person were viewed as fully competent then any healthcare interventions against their will would be unethical.

A clear issue with this approach is that the boundaries between mental health, disorder and illness are contentious. Continuum and dichotomous models are both advocated in this area. The latter stressing that specific forms of mental disorders are distinct, and may not be appropriately seen as extensions of normal behaviour (Horwitz and Scheid,

1999). Such dichotomous approaches generally derive from biological models and typically stress the organic basis of such disorders.

By contrast it is rare that 'mental health' is addressed in such models. Indeed, it is suggested by some that a definition of 'mental health' is not logically possible (Mechanic, 1999). Some aspects of good mental health have though been suggested. In a review of the area (Horowitz and Scheid, 1999) suggest such things as self-esteem, realisation of potential, the ability to maintain meaningful and fulfilling relations and psychological well-being can be viewed as central to good mental health. Others have suggested that psychological well-being can be divided into areas such as a sense of competence, the ability to manage aspects of the world, having a purpose in life and having the capacity for personal growth (Ryff, 1989). Mental health is clearly seen as more than the absence of 'mental disorder'.

Current practice based on this model has tended to advocate use of broad-based approaches which address a wide range of mental health problems, as well as specific forms of 'mental illness'. They have also increasingly come to recognise major changes in the rates of suicide have been the result of social and economic upheavals more than individual psychopathology (Hawton, 1994).

Even so research in this tradition has often reported high rates of specific mental disorders amongst those taking their own lives, sometimes exceeding 90 per cent (e.g. Barraclough, Bunch, Nelson et al, 1974). Many of these studies suffer from serious methodological weaknesses. For example, many have used retrospective identification of disorders such as depression. These have often been based on interviews conducted with friends and relatives. This introduces many sources of potential bias from relatives, friends and researchers.

More convincing research support for an association between suicide and mental disorder comes from studies using standardised mortality ratios (SMRs). These can be used to compare expected mortality rates by suicide of those with specific forms of disorder with the observed mortality rates. For those diagnosed before their death as having affective disorders such as depression and bipolar disorder, these comparisons suggest considerably more deaths by suicide than would be expected.

Similarly, those with a history of identified substance abuse also show similarly elevated levels of suicide.

Several international research studies have shown correlations between a broad range of mental health problems and subsequent suicide. The picture though is complicated and may involve the presence of multiple mental health issues prior to suicide. The role of mental health may also differ for various groups. For example, for young people completing suicide substance abuse, 'personality disorders' and difficult adjustment reactions have been reported to be frequently seen alongside depression (Hawton, 1994).

There are several criticisms of this group of approaches to suicide. Critically psychiatric models of mental disorder have traditionally emphasised precise description and classification of disorders. This is based on the observation of what are felt to be common features. This is common to most of medicine and indeed much of the biological and physical sciences. These approaches have come to be increasingly codified in recent years leading to the development of diagnostic frameworks. Widely used of these include DSM V (American Psychiatric Association, 2015) which tends to be used in North America and ICD 10 (ICD, 1993) which tends to be used outside North America. Most recent work into the relationship between suicide and forms of mental disorder has drawn on such frameworks.

Most strikingly the diagnostic categories have been challenged in terms of whether they can be reliably identified, and whether they in fact refer to valid categories. An example of a study in this area (Brockington, Kendell and Leff, 1978) looked at ten widely accepted operational definitions of schizophrenia, a defined form of mental disorder. The researchers used these on a sample of 119 people identified as being mentally disordered. The number defined as falling into the schizophrenic category varied from 3 to 45, depending on the definition used. This is further complicated in the context of forensic practice in criminal and civil justice settings. Here it is not uncommon for the emphasis to move from disorder to issues of 'personality disorder'. In moral terms this can be seen to involve a shift from notions of 'illness' to 'badness'.

Psychotic disorders

These are the group of mental disorders that are most central to medical models of mental disorder. They would typically include schizophrenia, affective psychoses, bipolar disorders, severe depression. It would also include psychosis due to known organic causes such as mercury poisoning. Psychotic disorders occurring in the absence of any known organic cause have been termed 'functional psychoses'.

The main characteristics of psychotic disorders are the presence of delusions and hallucinations (often called positive symptoms). What have been called negative symptoms may also be observed, and these would include such behaviours as social withdrawal, poor self-care and so on (Crow, 1985).

Personality disorders

A considerable portion of mental disorders is comprised of what have been termed 'personality disorders'. The definition of these is even more problematic than for psychotic disorders.

As can be seen from *Table 1*, DSM V and ICD 10 both provide coding systems for 'personality disorders'. The approach has generated considerable disagreement for many reasons. The use of a dichotomous approach to personality characteristics has been persuasively challenged on both theoretical and pragmatic grounds (Kinderman, 2015).

Linked to this the reliability and validity of such classifications of personality are poor. This perhaps accounts for the changing nature of the definitions used. Despite such revisions, the ability to consistently identify these personality types has not improved markedly. In response, it can be argued that the categories do capture aspects of interpersonal functioning. Some of these appear to be associated with difficulties for the individual and those around them. Some also appear to be correlated with suicide whilst others appear to act protectively.

Such medical models have had a marked impact on suicide research. They have certainly played a part in removing the stigma associated with suicide and mobilising resources to help those at risk. The philosophical and empirical basis of these approaches is not though strong. Many of the concepts used are problematic. The role of mental disorder and its association with suicide is not clear cut and has become increasingly controversial.

ICD 10	DSM V
Paranoid	Paranoid
Schizoid	Schizoid
	Schizotypal
Dissocial	Antisocial
Emotionally unstable Impulsive type	
Emotionally unstable Borderline type	Borderline
Histrionic	Histrionic
	Narcissistic
Anxious (avoidant)	Avoidant
Dependent	Dependent
Anankastic (Obsessive-Compulsive)	Obsessive- Compulsive
	Not otherwise specified

Table 1: Classification of Personality Disorders

Social Models of Suicide

Social models, in seeking to account for suicide, stress the external context in which the person finds themselves. Probably the most influential of these approaches to suicide has been the ground-breaking work of Durkheim (1952). This approach provided a basis for a large body of the subsequent research in this area. In his work, Durkheim rejected those approaches which attributed suicide to what he called 'extra-social' factors. For Durkheim, these including the medical models that attributed suicide to mental disorder. It also extended to explanations that were based on notions of race, heredity, climate and imitation.

In contrast Durkheim, related changes in suicide rates to social and economic forces that impinged on a person's life. This led him to argue that the stronger the social forces that pressed people back onto a dependence on their individual resources, the higher the suicide rate was likely to be. An example of this, given by Durkheim, was the Protestant Christian tradition. This form of Christian belief placed a greater stress on individualism than other forms of the religion. This he suggested was largely the explanation for higher suicide rates within this group, when compared to Catholic Christians.

Within his account, Durkheim also stressed the role of integration into a wider social life. This included family life but also extended to wider communities. Good levels of integration were for him critical determinants of suicide rates. This hypothesis receives support from other research. For example, the work of Brown and Prudo (1981) looked at the impact of community integration and found that those who were well integrated appeared to enjoy better mental health. Likewise, the suicide rates in the UK fell during major wars, when efforts to develop and maintain community integration were marked, but rose again in peacetime.

In developing his account of suicide Durkheim (1952) went on to suggest that there were three main types of suicide.

  (i)   Egoistic suicide. Which is seen where an individual's level of integration into social and family life is slight.
  (ii) Altruistic suicide. Which is seen in response to a perceived higher goal, and often occurs where individuals are overly integrated into social and/or familial life.
  (iii) Anomic suicide. Which he suggested followed a sudden broadening or narrowing of social horizons.

Durkheim also accepted the possibility of mixed types of suicide, specifically 'ego-anomic', 'altruistic-anomic' and 'ego-altruistic'.

It has been suggested by later researchers that, for Durkheim, suicide and crime were not an indication of immorality. Rather a given level of suicide (or crime) was to be expected in particular types of society. Where the rate showed rapid increases though, it was symptomatic of what has been termed the breakdown of collective conscience and fundamental flaws in the social system (Durkheim, 1952). It might be argued that this view has clear echoes when dramatic rises in suicide in prisons, as happened between 2010 and 2017 in the UK, are seen.

The approach advocated by Durkheim and later researchers adopting this approach, is clearly antithetical to models of suicide based on notions of mental disorder. In the 1950s Durkheim noted that no form of psychopathology showed a clear and consistent relationship to suicide. He also suggested that the number of suicides in each society did not vary in accordance with the number of those with mental disorders, however broadly defined. He did though appear to accept that those with better mental health may be protected against broader societal effects.

It is perhaps worth stressing that Durkheim discussed the broad range of psychological problems that an individual may face, as well as the more formal definitions of 'mental illness' and disorder that were then in place. Notwithstanding the stress on this at the time, he went on to argue that psychological difficulties alone do not fully account for the rate of suicide. Indeed, he saw such difficulties as largely secondary to social organization. This view still has considerable veracity and the notion that social and psychological factors interact in a complex manner, has become a foundation of much current thinking on suicide and related behaviours.

Additionally, Durkheim was dismissive of then popular notions of 'contagion' or 'imitation' as an explanation of suicide. He was dismissive of notions that suicide could be due to a process of contagion and imitation, arguing that the persistence of such views was implausible and lacking any experimental proof.

The work of Durkheim is important in several key respects. Most notably it provided a theory of what caused suicide. It also went beyond being simply descriptive but was genuinely a theoretical explanation. As such it gave rise to many testable hypotheses. Thus, the theory gave rise to many empirical studies, even though Durkheim himself was sceptical of the value of such approaches to understanding the motivations to suicide. Some of his scepticism appears to have been based on the poor quality of information available to him in this area, in the late 19th and early-20th Centuries.

The quality of empirical information available today is now much improved. However, it is unlikely that this would fully address Durkheim's concerns about empiricism.

It can also be reasonably argued that Durkheim's approach gave rise to concepts of 'partial suicide'. By this he meant self-destructive or self-punishing behaviours that did not result in death, suggesting that such behaviours may form part of a continuum. Such notions were in turn influenced by psychoanalytic thinking and the views of suicide and self-injury derived from this (Walsh and Rosen, 1988). It is therefore surprising that sociological and psychoanalytic approaches to suicide developed in parallel, but in relative isolation from each other. There have been few attempts to integrate these approaches, although there are some notable exceptions (e.g. Menninger, 1938).

The central criticism of these approaches to suicide has been the challenge of relating individual difficulties, and actions, to the social environments that in turn may serve to induce or aggravate suicidal risk.

Psychological theories of suicide

Like the work of Durkheim, modern psychological theories of suicide can be traced back primarily to the work of Freud. This essentially posited an instinctive drive towards self-destruction, which in turn needed to be controlled (Lester, 1991). As in other areas the work of Freud and his successors provided a theoretical model which, in turn, generated many testable hypotheses. It can also be criticised as having generated many untestable hypotheses, making the theory closed to refutation. Psychological models have also been applied to this approach to suicide. Psychological models of 'mental disorder' have resulted in a distinct approach. These models have questioned the dichotomous view of notions such as 'personality disorder', 'mental illness' (e.g. schizophrenia) other forms of mental health problems (e.g. substance abuse).

Psychological models are particularly well developed in the study of depression and depressed mood. Because of this the area of depression is discussed in detail. However, similar arguments can and have been applied to a range other forms of mental health problems (Towl, 1996; 1997).

Psychological models of depression differ from psychiatric models in generally seeing affective state as part of a continuum, without the clear dichotomies suggested by the diagnostic systems such as DSM IV or ICD-10 discussed above.

Cognitive models of depressed mood

Cognitive approaches to depressed mood have in recent years focussed primarily on the role of 'patterns' of thinking and the influence of 'life events'. Beck (1967) argued that depressed mood is, largely, a function of the way a person thinks about the world. He suggested that some, due to a combination of predisposition and early experiences, are particularly prone to what he termed 'negative automatic thoughts' (e.g. the idea that events will always turn out badly). Linked to this, he suggested that those who show depressed mood tend to consistently and repeatedly make logical errors in their thinking. Examples here would include the belief that they must always do things perfectly. Beck described such thoughts as illogical on the basis that they were unattainable. Anyone holding such belief would, he suggested, rapidly become disappointed with their own performance measured against such unattainable criteria. Such 'failures' to achieve their own illogical expectations would lead to feelings of depression.

In a later study (Beck, Kovacs and Weissman, 1979) it was suggested that multiple developmental factors might predispose a person towards dysfunctional patterns of thinking. The authors suggested that these included:

(i)   Experiencing tangible losses such as the death of a caretaker during childhood.

(ii) Developing expectations of loss both real and imagined.

(iii) Experiences that served to lower self-esteem both real or imagined, for example experiencing being bullied or having feelings of being unwanted.

(iv) Experiencing sudden marked reversals in social status or valuation.

Sociobiological approaches

Sociobiology is an area of research that stresses the relationship between evolutionary theory and behaviour (Wilson, 2000). This theory suggests many forms of behaviour can be explained by their tendency to increase reproductive success of genes rather than individuals. The theory has addressed the issue of why apparently dysfunctional behaviours are seen and seen across all known human societies. This has included efforts to account for experiences such as depression and other mental disorders, as well as the tendency towards the destructive behaviours, towards self and others, suggested in psychoanalytic theories. Research in this area has served to undermine historic notions that suicide is in some sense unnatural or that it runs counter to biological 'laws'. Some work in this area provides support for a tendency towards self-destructive behaviour and seeks to explain this in terms of its effects beyond the individual (Wilson, 2000). It is important to stress here that just because a behaviour may be 'natural' this does not equate to it being moral or desirable. Theorists in this area often quote the example of violence. This may convey biological advantages in terms of survival and reproductive success. It is in this sense 'natural'. Equally it is generally seen as immoral and warranting strong efforts to prevent and reduce its occurrence. Arguably, the main contribution of sociobiological approaches has been to suggest the basis for the kind of vulnerability to self-destructive behaviours identified in psychoanalytic and other theories of suicide.

Life events research

There is an extensive body of research looking at the effects of social context on depression (Brown and Harris, 1978). This is often termed 'life events' research and the study by Brown and Harris illustrates this approach. It looked at the effects of life events on 458 women living in an inner-city area in England. They found that 114 of their sample went on to show evidence of depression during their study, with most receiving medical treatment in the form of drug-based treatment. A smaller number were also admitted to mental hospitals for treatment. It was reported that 'severe life events' such as loss of housing, were four times as likely to be seen in those who became depressed (Brown and Harris,

1993). Several characteristics also appeared to be related to an increased risk of becoming depressed. These included having three or more children under 14 years living at home, being of lower socio-economic status, loss of the woman's own mother early in life and being unemployed. Subsequent work in this area has tended to confirm these findings and noted many 'protective factors' in the social environment. For example, Harris and Brown noted that those women who had at least one close and supportive relationship appeared to be largely protected from feelings of depression (Lin, Dean and Ensel, 2013).

Diathesis-stress research

Current psychological models of suicide have primarily involved 'diathesis-stress' models. The term diathesis here refers to a pre-existing weakness or vulnerability. Stress relates to perceived difficulty in meeting demands faced by the person. Such vulnerability it is suggested may become critical when activated by stress. Many accounts of this type have been developed with a similar theoretical basis (Schneidman, 1985; Schotte and Clum, 1987; Wenzel and Beck, 2008; Williams, Van der Does, Barnhofer et al, 2008; O'Connor, 2011).

The psychological model of suicide developed by Shneidman (1985; 1987) gives a clear sense of this theoretical approach and has been built on by later researchers. The model starts by clearly recognising the role of psychological distress in suicide. Suicide is viewed as an attempt to solve problems that a person faces. Likewise, suicide is seen to be an attempt to resolve problems that are causing intense psychological suffering. In this respect suicide is viewed as a continuation from normal psychological processes, rather than being distinct and qualitatively different. Based on this Schneidman argued that suicidal behaviour tends to have several common themes. Firstly, he argued that nearly all suicides will have the purpose of seeking a solution to specific problems. In addition, there will be a behavioural goal in suicide of cessation of consciousness. The stimulus for suicide it is suggested is intolerable psychological pain, precipitated by the psychological stressor of frustrated psychological needs. The emotional experience Schneidman suggested is one of both hopelessness and helplessness but the cognitive state experienced is one of ambivalence. The perceptual state it is suggested is one of narrowing of the ability to see alternative options. In turn this leads to aggression. The interpersonal action suggested is one of communication of intention. Finally, it was suggested that a high degree of consistency would typically be present, in line with a lifelong pattern of adaptive styles (Crighton and Towl, 1997)

As outlined, Shneidman's model of suicide seeks to explain completed suicide within a clear psychological framework. The model served to generate empirically testable ideas and several these have received empirical support from research studies. For example, the suggestion that consistent patterns of ineffective problem-solving behaviours, coupled to high levels of hopelessness and helplessness, has received support (MacLeod, Williams and Linehan, 1992).

Later models have sought to build and elaborate on such ideas. For example, Joiner (2005) outlines an interpersonal theory of suicide. This suggests that the co-existence of feelings of being a burden and not belonging are central to suicide. When these are marked, they lead to increasing feelings of hopelessness. For Joiner (2005) this is likely to progress to suicide only where the person acquires capability to complete suicide, involving reduced fear of death and increased tolerance of pain. Here previous experience of violence may serve to increase capacity, as would acts of self-injury. Notions of belonging echo the views of Durkheim and the findings of Brown and Harris and others, on the powerful effects of social context on suicide. It is perhaps not difficult to see why prisons create risks in this area.

It is important to note that psychological models of this type see suicide as clearly as a form of behaviour, explicable in similar terms to functional behaviours. In this respect suicide and indeed self-injury is not seen as an effect resulting from the presence of some form of mental disorder. It can be argued that only in recent years have concerted efforts been made to develop psychological and psychosocial models of this type to explain suicidal behaviour. Such models draw from what is currently known about behaviour and particularly human cognition. The approach has contrasted markedly with the psychiatric approach described above, where suicidal behaviour is generally seen as the product of an underlying 'illness' such as depression.

A theoretical model of suicide in prisons

Few efforts have been made to develop theoretical models of suicide in prison. Early research was understandably descriptive in nature. More recent work has continued to be descriptive, with some focus on the identification of risk and protective factors. An exception to this has been the application of a model based on the series of studies conducted in the 1990s (e.g. Crighton and Towl, 1997; Towl and Crighton, 1998). This theoretical model built on the work of Plutchik (1997) and his collaborators. It aimed to link fundamental psychological research into emotions, to the behaviour of suicide and indeed various forms of intentional self-injury seen in prisons. Specifically, the model suggested an explicit relationship between the emotional state of anger and a variety of forms of self-destructive behaviour.

It can be argued that such a link is especially apposite in relation to suicides in prison. In adopting a scientific approach such theoretical models are central to understanding. They are also central to making progress by generating testable, and therefore potentially refutable, hypotheses. Accurate observation and recording of information is of course an important part of developing an understanding of an area of study. On its own though it is severely limited and produces diminishing returns. There is a strong argument to be made that work on suicides in prisons had become largely moribund in the absence of credible theoretical work.

Methodological issues

Previous research into the area of suicides in prisons can be criticised as failing to address key methodological challenges. Some of these are inherent to this area of research. They are not though unique to suicides in prisons and many are common to studies of suicide in the community as well, where they have been more effectively addressed.

A detailed review of this area is provided by Rothman and Greenland (1998) looking at the broad field of epidemiological research.

Causation

The issue of causation is difficult in the context of suicide. Our ideas about causation develop from early infancy onwards and, in practical terms, simple causal models allow us to function in our physical and social worlds. Scientific theories of causation are though more complex than this and our intuitive models may serve to systematically mislead us. For example, the concept of causation developed early in life assumes direct correspondence between observed cause and effect. People normally see each cause as itself being necessary and sufficient to give an effect. When we press a light switch this appears to be the singular cause of the light going on. This is of course not correct (Rothman and Greenland, 1998). A 'sufficient cause' is in fact, one which provides the minimal set of conditions for an event to happen.

Epidemiological research into suicide has arguably tended toward attributions of overall levels of risk to groups. This is typically stated in terms of overall morbidity and mortality. This reflects our inability to measure individual risks, therefore leading to us giving average values to all those in a category. In turn this reflects ignorance of the determinants of suicide and the way these interact.

Strength and interaction of effects

In epidemiology, the strength of an effect is usually measured by the change in frequency of an event that follows introduction of a given factor in a population. For any causal mechanism, its components causes may have strong or weak effects. This is further complicated in that the strength of effects for components may change over time. An important implication of this is that causation is not a static thing. It will change over time.

Component causes in turn may interact. This suggests that different causal factors may yield the same sufficient cause for an event. These interactions may occur at the same time but they may also be temporally distant from each other. To take an example from the prison context, having a family visit delayed or refused may be temporally distant from a suicide. It may also be a causal factor interacting with feelings of hopelessness and helplessness.

Some researchers have been highly critical of early research into suicide which, they argue, was based on a false premise that causal factors should sum to 100 per cent. This accounts in large part for the arguments around whether 'depression' or some other factor is the main cause of suicides. As noted above causal factors may interact and this implies that such factors need not sum to 100 per cent. It has been stressed that the upper limit under these conditions for all the component causes of all the causal mechanisms is in fact infinity not 100 per cent. It is only that fraction attributable to a single component cause that will not exceed 100 per cent (Rothman and Greenland, 1998).

Methodological problems in prison suicide

Many weaknesses have been identified in past research into prison suicides. In her research Liebling (1991) pointed out the reliance of early studies on written record. She also noted the lack of critical reflection in these studies on the quality of this data. In turn she noted five main difficulties with prior research:

(i)   the adequacy of figures on suicides;
(ii)   the inadequacy of incident figures on suicide attempts and self-injury;
(iii)   the lack of any control group;
(iv)   the inadequacy and inappropriateness of recorded information;
(v)   the focus on the prediction of the suicidal inmate.

These concerns have had varying levels of impact on research and some have gone on to be repeated.

A substantial amount of research into suicides in prisons has been predicated on the idea of continuity between different expressions of self-destructive feelings and behaviours (e.g. Jones, 1996). Within such a model levels of intentional self-injury are clearly relevant to suicide research, providing as they do a means to gain self-report data that would not otherwise be available. Others have rejected such continuity, stressing that suicide is distinct and different from self-injury (e.g. Kreitman, 1977). This school of thought suggests that there is, at some point, a clear discontinuity between suicidal and self-injurious behaviour. If correct this would suggest that the study of self-injury was of little or no relevance and may indeed be quite misleading as the behaviours have different functions to suicide. This type of data has though significantly influenced research and practice in relation to suicides in prisons. As noted above the relevance of information derived from studies of intentional self-injury to suicide remains hypothetical at this stage. Further research is required to demonstrate similarities or indeed differences between the two forms of behaviour.

The lack of control group data in suicide research is a complex methodological issue. For cases of completed suicide there is clearly no option but to get self-report information from the individual. It would also be completely unethical to conduct self-report studies on high-risk groups, without also actively intervening to reduce risk where this was felt to be high. Intervention would, in turn, throw into question any results from such studies. Researchers have therefore often resorted to simply describing the characteristics of those who kill themselves, without any reference to control data. Such results are of limited value in informing policy and practice in suicide prevention, since the characteristics described may simply be a facet of the prison population.

Similarities between suicide and suicide attempts

A community-based study by Sletten, Emerson and Brown (1973) suggested that 'suicide attempters' in the community resembled completed suicides. Similarities were reported across several diagnostic, demographic and familial variables. Another study (Sheiban, 1993) followed up 1,307 people who had attempted suicide, over a ten-year period. Here it was reported that 18 per cent of those who made multiple attempts went on to kill themselves.

Several smaller scale studies found similar results, with previous studies suggesting that the major risk factor increasing the risk of suicide is previous suicide attempts (Appleby, 1992; Appleby, Kapur, Shaw et al, 2015).

In reviewing this area of research Plutchik (1997) argued that there are major difficulties with such a simplistic approach to assessing risk. He suggested many problems with an approach based purely on identifying risk and protective factors in suicide and these are worth considering in some detail. Firstly, he noted that such an approach often looks at broad social and demographic variables such as sex, age and race. In turn these have little value in addressing predictions of individual behaviour. He was also critical of the tendency to assume that some variables such as depression, because they are found commonly in a suicidal population, are somehow more important in predicting outcome. Thirdly, he noted that the approach has no way of dealing with the finding that many people will have multiple risk factors yet will show no signs of suicidal thinking or behaviour (Plutchik, 1997)

What seems evident from the research is that multiple factors are interacting over time to lead to a suicidal event. Within such a multi-causal system efforts to suggest that one causal factor such as depression is primary, are entirely invalid. The situation may more appropriately be seen as similar to those non-linear systems studied within 'chaos theory'. Here a small event may trigger a cascade of events that lead to major events that are not predictable in simple ways (O'Carroll, 1993).

It has been convincingly suggested that multiple causation of suicide is now often formally recognised, but that the implications of this are poorly understood and applied into practice (O'Carroll, 1993). This is reflected in much of the evidence base that proposes that, for example, most suicides are caused by factor X (e.g. 'clinical depression'). Such themes recur and have influenced both research and practice. 'clinical depression' has often been seen as a prerequisite for completed suicide, with other causal factors being dismissed or downgraded.

Such propositions have led to largely futile disputes within suicide research between advocates of different risk (and to a lesser extent protective) factors, which they argue are central to suicide.

A related error in suicide research has been the notion that even where multiple causation is accepted, one factor must somehow be more causal than others. Returning to the example of switching on an electric light, the absurdity of this idea is perhaps made clear. Multiple causal factors can result in the light not coming on. The power station could have failed, the main grid may have failed, the bulb may be defective, the switch may be defective. The causal factors could be multiplied. It makes little sense though to suggest that one of these is somehow the most important one in preventing the light operating.

This is linked to another problem seen in the research, namely that of one-to-one causation. This view of causation holds that if a given factor is strongly associated with suicide this should be the focus of any intervention efforts. In relation to suicide this has often taken the form of 'clinical depression' being common in suicide, therefore 'treatment' of this should be the focus of efforts to reduce suicide. This does not logically follow. As O'Carroll (1993) noted prevention of suicides involves efforts to interrupt any of the causal elements that lead to that suicide being completed. The best points to intervene may or may not be the most obvious.

As with other forms of physical or psychological disorders, the task is further complicated by the variable temporal distance between causal factors and outcomes. The causal factors involved in a completed suicide may not be proximal in time to the event at all. People may follow various paths to the same destination.

This is perhaps best illustrated with concrete examples.

Case 1: A → B → C → D → Completed Suicide
- Where A might represent physical and/or sexual abuse in childhood.
- B Failure to identify or effectively intervene in A to mitigate the long term negative effects.
- C Experiences in later life that re-open these psychological wounds.
- D Failure of prison staff or other prisoners to recognise suicidal ideation.

Case 2: E → F → G → Completed Suicide
- E May be a recent divorcee.
- F Could be the absence of a social support network.
- G Could be a recent reception into prison.

There is often a tendency in the first example to see A as the 'primary' cause of the completed suicide in case 1. It is though also by far the most difficult to intervene with. As a response to this O'Carroll advocates a policy of breaking sequences at their weakest points, stressing the need to intervene at as many places as possible. Proximal factors are often the most obvious and therefore the focus of attention in research and practice. However, there may be other points in the sequence where interventions can be effective.

Finally, O'Carroll goes on to note the occurrence of common pathways to suicide. Thus, while there are very many possible pathways to a completed suicide, some pathways or patterns of causal elements appear to be more common. He gives the example of psychological states of hopelessness (Beck, 1967; Beck, Kovacs and Weissman, 1979). An observation that has also been made within the context of prisons (Dexter and Towl, 1995). This suggests that some interventions may have marked impacts on suicide rates by breaking common pathways.

O'Carroll goes on to suggest six points around suicide prevention:

(1) That interventions should focus on factors that have been shown to be causally related to suicide. This in turn causes problems since the evidence base is very poor, with most research to date looking at 'psychiatric' factors.

(2) That the strength of association of such factors with suicide, along with their prevalence in the population, are what will determine their public health importance.

(3) That researchers should seek to identify factors which are often necessary components and are common pathways to suicide.

(4) That the focus should be on events that are potentially modifiable.

(5) That the costs of intervention on a causal element should be compared with the costs of focusing on alternative elements of the causal mechanism.

(6) That efforts should be made to address as many causal elements as are vulnerable to intervention.

Overall it is clear that suicide is not an area where only one causal element can be addressed, therefore the need is to identify and address multiple elements.

Protective factors

Suicide research in prisons has generally not progressed much beyond the listing of risk factors. As noted by some researchers there has been little work on 'protective' factors in suicide (Crighton and Towl, 1997). Research in the community has progressed further in this respect, but as Plutchik (1997) noted, in respect of factors which protect against suicide, little of the research has gone beyond the notion of listing factors which may cancel out risk factors (e.g. good familial support). He suggests that there is now a clear need to go beyond this within a theoretical model of suicide.

He goes on to outline what he terms a 'two stage model of countervailing forces'. There is, Plutchik notes, considerable evidence that suicide and violent behaviour are correlated and co-occur. Around 30 per cent of violent individuals have a history of self-injurious behaviours and around 10–20 per cent of 'suicidal' people have a recorded history of violent behaviour (Skodal and Karasu, 1978). Such observations can be placed within a broad theoretical framework drawn from ethological and evolutionary psychology (now generally termed sociobiology). This is an approach that looks for broad, cross species, commonalties in behaviour. It seeks to tie behaviours such as suicide, attempted suicide and intentional self-injury, to fundamental research into human emotions.

In discussing the nature and role of emotions Plutchik (1994; 1997) suggested six central postulates:

(1) That emotions exist as communication and survival mechanisms, acting to signal intentions of future actions by means of a variety of behavioural displays.
(2) That emotions have a genetic basis.
(3) That emotions are hypothetical constructs based on various classes of evidence.

(4) That emotions are complex chains of events with stabilising feedback loops that serve to provide some kind of behavioural homeostasis.

(5) That the relations amongst emotions can be represented by a 3-dimensional structural model.

(6) That emotions are related to several derivative conceptual domains.

This model recognises that certain events may trigger a chain of events that are termed emotions. The events which trigger emotions in turn tend to be those which disrupt the equilibrium of the individual.

The model outlined suggests that many parts of the process are not open to conscious appraisal. This reflects the fact that individuals will often have little insight into their physical states, or the functions being served by their emotions. This in turn has important implications. Emotional states will be inferences or guesses that necessarily draw on limited data. Hence everyone will try to interpret not only the emotions of others but also their own emotions (Plutchik, 1993).

A further implication of the model has direct relevance for intervention, as it implies a role for cognitive determination in subsequent emotion. This suggests that intervention here may serve to alter or mute emotional states.

A common emotional state is anger and the behavioural expression of this is aggression. Ethological views of aggression see it as serving many positive functions such as increasing access to resources, dealing with conflicts between individuals and increasing the chances of reproduction. By increasing the chances of individual survival and reproduction, some degree of aggression is therefore selected for in future generations.

There is also considerable neurophysiological evidence of structures within the brain geared primarily to aggressive behaviour (i.e. lateral hypothalamus, ventral segmental area, mid-brain central grey area, and the central and anterior portions of the septum). Some neurotransmitters also appear to be closely involved in such behaviour. For example, animals fed on a tryptophan free diet show increased aggressive behaviour, suggesting that low levels of serotonin are associated with aggression.

Plutchik goes on to argue that suicide can be usefully viewed as a derived form of aggressive behaviour.

The two-stage model of suicide

Within this model aggression is defined as a theoretical inner state, whilst violence refers to the overt behaviour resulting from such an inner state. There are various types of 'life events' that have been shown to increase aggressive impulses. These would include threats, challenges, changes in hierarchical status, loss of social attachments, physical pain, loss of power or respect, amongst many others.

Whether aggression goes on to be overtly expressed will depend on many factors; some of which will serve to amplify and some attenuate the aggressive impulse. Whether aggression will be seen will depend on the balance and interaction of these factors at a given time. Within the process Plutchik referred to what he called 'amplifiers' and 'attenuators' as 'Stage I countervailing forces'. The term amplifiers here referred to events serving to increase the likelihood of aggressive behaviour resulting in violence, whilst attenuators referred to events decreasing this likelihood. The complex interaction of both, rather than simple additive processes was stressed.

Overt action also requires a goal to be directed towards. The model assumes that some variables will result in violence being directed towards self, and some will result in its direction towards others. Violence may also have a negative feedback function, in that violence towards others may serve to reduce the threat from them. Suicidal acts may serve as a call for help, or create guilt in others, both of which may help in managing a crisis or unsatisfactory relationships. The use of violent behaviour can therefore function as a feedback system which aims to keep social interactions within certain limits. This process is the same as occurs in other emotional reactions, so bringing the study of suicide within the general study of emotion.

Applying the theory

Plutchik et al(1989) went on to developed a Suicide Risk Scale (SRS). This was based largely on two findings. One that those who have made previous suicide attempts are at increased risk. The second that the presence of more risk factors results in increased levels of risk. These findings parallel other epidemiological research.

The model is vectoral, meaning that different factors may contribute in an additive way, but with different possible weights. Where the contribution of 'amplifiers' is greater than that of 'attenuators' then overt behaviour will be displayed. In turn, different variables will then determine the expression of that overt behaviour once a threshold is exceeded. Plutchik terms these factors as 'Stage II countervailing forces'.

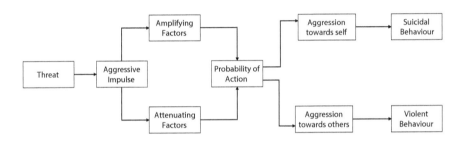

Figure 1: A model of suicidal and violent behaviour in prisons

Some implications of the model

Many testable hypotheses emerge from this theoretical model. In this way, it provides a framework for useful further research, which goes beyond the purely descriptive. In linking to the fundamental research the model also suggests the fundamental basis for suicidal behaviour, locating this in the neuropsychological basis of emotion.

The model also suggests several practical implications. Most strikingly from the perspective of research into prison suicide, it suggests that suicide and violence are not clearly separate behaviours. Violence towards others and towards ourselves are viewed as alternative expressions of common emotional states. The nature of the expression being largely dependent on social context. The theoretical model locates both behaviours as part of the same behavioural system. Thus, it would be hypothesised interventions that successfully reduce the risk of violence towards others are likely to reduce suicide risk, and vice versa.

A second key implication of the model is that attempts to assess the risk of suicide and the risk of violence should go together, as they draw on the same emotional 'system'.

Advocates of this approach also stressed the importance of moving beyond a simple identification of risk and protective factors. A clear distinction was drawn between amplifiers and attenuators in the context of the theory and the study of risk and protective factors. It was argued that risk and protective factors are simply descriptive statements of positive or negative correlations of variables with an outcome measure such as suicide. In contrast, it was suggested that amplifiers and attenuators were theoretical terms embedded in a broader evolutionary theory of emotion and the use of aggression in the regulation of inter-personal relationships (Plutchik et al, 1989).

Finally, the model suggests that there are potentially a very large number of variables that might influence suicide and violence. Thus, it was argued that research in this area should not be limited to the traditional sociological, demographic and 'diagnostic' variables that had been the focus of attention. Stress on the role of depression was challenged on the basis that other variables had been identified as correlating with suicide risk as high or higher than depression. These variables included the number of life problems a person had, their score on the MMPI schizophrenia scale scores, dyscontrol scores, the presence of recent psychiatric symptoms, estimates of passivity, the total number of family problems, impulsivity and poor reality testing. It seems likely that many others may be relevant in the risk of suicide in prisons but that they have simply not been looked for. Such observations it was suggested supported the notion that too much attention on only a few variables in research into suicide (Plutchik, 1997).

It seems clear that such a model is of relevance to the study of suicide in general, in that it provides a scientifically testable explanatory framework. This theoretical model therefore serves at least three key functions. Firstly, it serves to generate testable hypotheses in relation to suicide. For example, that those who show high levels of aggression will also show high levels of suicide and intentional self-injury. Secondly, the model provides a framework for integrating empirical and non-empirical observations relating to suicide. Thirdly, it serves to link applied research into suicides to fundamental research into emotions, yielding explanations that go beyond simple patterns of correlations.

Research into suicide in prisons has primarily been concerned with making empirical and non-empirical observations but in the absence of any clear theoretical framework to guide and support such observations. It can also be convincingly argued that research in prisons has shown a marked tendency to look for a single or small number of 'causes' of suicides in prison; in much the same way as community-based research (Dexter and Towl, 1994; Crighton, 1997; Crighton and Towl, 1997). Rarely have theoretical models been suggested but they have tended to be of very limited explanatory power, and to have been poorly integrated with fundamental research.

The two-stage model seems especially valuable in attempting to develop future studies of suicide in prisons, since these institutions contain large numbers of individuals with a history of aggression and violence towards themselves and others. Prisons may also provide a particularly good setting in which to test aspects of this model, informing subsequent policy and practice.

CHAPTER 3

Community Research into Suicide

Introduction

Prisons are clearly not separate from the wider community that they serve. This fact is central to understanding the area of suicide in prisons. Prisoners are drawn from and normally return to the wider community. They are not though a random cross-section of society and some groups are much more likely to find themselves in prison custody. Because of this wider social and public health trends in society are important to understanding suicide in prisons, in a manner that goes beyond simple comparisons of rates of death.

In reviewing the research on suicide in the community the aim is to draw out studies that are methodologically sophisticated, as well as those which are most relevant to understanding suicides in the context of prison custody. Such a review is necessarily highly selective. The focus is therefore largely on studies conducted in the United Kingdom.

Defining suicide in the community

Early research into suicide was often based on analyses of legally defined suicides. In turn this led to the introduction of several systematic biases, because of the legal criteria used. The Suicide Act 1961 removed the act of suicide from the criminal calendar of offences in the UK so far as the person attempting suicide is concerned. Prior to this though, an act of attempted suicide was a criminal offence (it remains an offence to assist someone to commit suicide). Before 1961, in law suicide was seen essentially as an act of self-murder and required a criminal level of proof. Community-based data before 1961 is therefore difficult to interpret, as there was most probably a tendency for under-reporting and, in addition, there was a strong legal presumption against suicide. Whilst suicide is no longer a criminal offence, the legal presumption against suicide verdicts remains and as a result many self-inflicted deaths may go on to be recorded as 'open' or 'misadventure' verdicts by coroners, where the act cannot be proved beyond reasonable doubt.

Within the UK, Scotland has a separate legal system and has adopted a different system of legally examining deaths. In Scotland, the Police Service has greater responsibility in determining whether deaths are natural, self-inflicted or suspicious. The presumptions against suicide though appear to be just as strong as in other parts of and nations within the UK.

Studies of suicide in the community in the UK have therefore needed to address these effects. One approach has been to use operational definitions of suicide drawn from the broader public health field. These differ significantly from the legal definitions of suicide. Generally these have drawn on the definitions of causes of death, as set out in the International Classification of Diseases (ICD) (ICD, 1993). This approach has a number of significant advantages, including the fact that it will capture a larger group of self-inflicted deaths. In doing this it removes some of the biases inherent in the legal processes. Finally, it allows for valid comparisons to be made across different legal jurisdictions by comparing similar behaviours.

Epidemiological studies

A major epidemiological study of suicide in the community was conducted by Charlton et al(1992a; 1992b). This involved analysis of suicides in England and Wales covering the period 1911 to 1990. In addition, a further analysis of suicides and undetermined deaths covering the period 1963 to 1990 was conducted. It remains a highly influential study which impacted on policy and practice in the community, as well as the methodology of subsequent work in this area.

The authors used operational definitions based on the 6th revision of the ICD framework. Specifically, they adopted two definitions of 'suicide' described as:

(a)   *recorded suicides*: 6th ICD E970-E979; 7th ICD E970-E979, 8th ICD 950-E959; 9th ICD E950-E959 (as used in population trends 35[2]); and

(b)   *suicides and undetermined* (from 1968 onwards only): as (a) above plus E980-E989, excluding E988.8 after 1978.

(Charlton et al, 1992a)

Using these defintions, three year moving averages for rates of death were calculated. The authors noted a marked reduction in the number of suicides during the First and Second World Wars, along with marked increases during the inter-war period of economic depression which peaked in 1932. They also noted an upward trend following World War II, where suicides for men and women rose to a peak in 1963. Over this time the increase for women was greater than that for men.

After 1963 they noted that the rate of suicide for women began a sustained decline, which continued to the end of 1990. A similar decrease in the rates for suicides and undetermined deaths was seen, leading the researchers to suggest this was a genuine decrease and not a result of lower recording of suicide deaths.

Suicide rates for men showed a similar pattern from 1963 until the 1970s. After this point though the trends clearly diverged. For men, the rate of suicides and suicides and undetermined deaths rose in parallel from the 1970s to the 1990s. This was noted to be the first time since 1911 that male and female suicide trends had moved in opposite directions.

A further analysis of suicide rates (1946–90) and suicides and undetermined deaths (1968–90) was conducted, using five-year age cohorts. For men, the suicide rates had tended to converge for all age groups by 1986–90. The one exception to this was the 15–24 age group, where there had been a significant rise in the suicide rate. The rate for this group remained markedly lower than for the older age groups of men but the difference had reduced. For women, a similar pattern of convergence was seen. Here though it was in a downward direction towards lower rates of self-inflicted deaths. Again the 15–24 age group proved to be an exception and here the rates did not decline but remained unchanged.

The rates for this group were though markedly lower than for older age cohorts of women.

The researchers went on to consider whether the changes observed in suicide and undetermined death rates could be accounted for as an age cohort effect. In men, they noted that more recent cohorts had higher age for age mortality rates than earlier ones. The 1966 cohort had higher mortality than the 1956 one, which in turn had higher mortality than the 1946 one. Their 1971 cohort had a mortality rate at ages 15–19 of 52 deaths per million of population, which is significantly higher than for all earlier cohorts at this age. They also noted that the suicide rates in the cohorts born after 1946 may not yet have peaked, in which case it may have been expected the suicide rates of the under 45 age group would continue to rise for some years. The earlier cohorts displayed a different pattern. The 1916 cohorts had a pronounced peak at age 45–9 (the 1960s peak). The 1936 and 1962 cohorts had peaks at age 45–49 and 55–59 respectively that corresponded to deaths in the early 1980s.

For women aged 45 and over it can clearly be seen how successive birth cohorts experienced lower age for suicide mortality. The 1936 cohort had lower rates of self-inflicted deaths than the 1926 cohort, which in turn had lower rates than the 1916 cohort. Below age 45 the picture is similar apart from a marked increase in the 1960s. The 1966 cohort had lower rates than the 1956 cohort, which in turn had lower rates than the 1946 cohort.

The researchers concluded that there was evidence of both cohort and period effects on suicide rates in men and women.

Method of self-inflicted death

Few differences were reported between age groups in the methods used. Clear period effects were seen though. For example, in the period 1948–50 poisoning by domestic gas accounted for 41 per cent of deaths of men and 60 per cent of deaths for women. The advent of natural gas greatly reduced the prevalence of this method of suicide. By 1968–70 poisoning by solid or liquid substances had become the most used method, especially for women, accounting for around two thirds of recorded suicides. During the 1988–90 period this remained the most common method used by women. For men, though, poisoning by other gases, predominantly car exhaust gases, took over and accounted for around one third of recorded suicides. The use of hanging also increased for men. For the period 1948–50 this accounted for around 20 per cent of recorded suicides. By 1988–90 this had increased to 31 per cent. The figures for women were eight per cent and 25 per cent respectively.

Rates of poisoning from gases other than domestic gas has increased from very low levels in the 1948–50 period, to become one of the most common methods of self-inflicted death in the community. Unlike other methods it is less common in the over 65 age group. In 1988–90 the 15–44 age group showed the highest rate for this method. During the 1980s more than 90 per cent of such deaths were due to motor vehicle exhaust gas. Such changes have clearly been influenced by the very marked increase in motor vehicle ownership and greater access to motor vehicles generally. This method was though much less common in women.

The researchers noted that recorded rates of suicide by poisoning increased for all age groups between 1948–50 to 1963–65, followed by a decrease, especially in those aged over 45. Suicide rates by this method are generally higher for women than for men and are highest in the over 65 age group (more than twice the rate for the 15–44 age group).

The authors report a particularly marked increase over the period studied, in hanging and suffocation as a cause of self-inflicted death in young men (defined as under 30 years). The authors note a tendency for women to use suffocation as a method, rather than hanging. Nearly 90 per cent of recorded suicide deaths in men in this group were by hanging. For women, in contrast this peaked at around 60 per cent by 1990.

Amongst other methods seen were death by trauma following jumps from high places. This was seen at similar levels in both sexes but was more common in younger age groups. Self-inflicted death using firearms or explosives were more commonly seen in men. Whilst drowning was more commonly seen in the over 45 age group.

Deaths by region

Charlton et al(1992a) went on to compare suicides and undetermined deaths for men and women aged 15–44 (including ICD code E988.8).

They compared two time periods, 1979–83 and 1985–9 across health authority regions, looking at suicides and suicides plus undetermined deaths. They reported that both definitions yielded similar patterns of results and they therefore reported data based on the broader definition including undetermined deaths.

They reported that South East Thames, North West and East Anglia Regional Health Authorities (RHAs) had the highest rates of self-inflicted deaths at 225, 218 and 209 deaths per million of population respectively. Oxford, North East Thames, Wessex, Merseyside and Yorkshire had the lowest rates—all around 160 per million of population.

The suicide rates in young men were found to have increased across all the regions studied. By far the largest increase was seen in the East Anglia region with a 58 per cent increase. Large increases of 25 per cent or more were also seen in the North West, Oxford and Trent regions.

Women in South East Thames and North West Thames regions were found to have the highest rates at 85 and 71 per million of population respectively. The lowest rates for women were found in the Trent region (47) and in Wales (48). All the regional rates for women had decreased, except for South East Thames, East Anglia and Oxford. North West Thames had shown the largest decrease (29 per cent), followed by Wales (17 per cent).

Factors associated with self-inflicted deaths.

The researchers went on to suggest several factors which might be associated with suicide and undetermined deaths in the community. These included the presence of illness, both physical and mental. Within this they included substance use problems involving alcohol and other drugs. They also suggested that social factors such as the level of social cohesion and support, as well as attitudes towards suicide were important.

At a broader level, they suggested that stressful life events, including such things as unemployment, divorce, widowhood, imprisonment, migration, diagnosis of threatening illness, traumatic shock, and involvement in war were important. In addition, they noted the role of wider cultural changes in society and changes in the economic climate and access to means of suicide.

Population data of this type is of limited explanatory power in accounting for individual deaths. The researchers noted that the probability of an individual ending their life was dependent on multiple effects happening in combination. Equally it is worth noting that risk and protective factors will act in interaction around and before the time of the event. With aggregation of data Charlton et al(1992b) noted that changes in different individual factors may be masked by the level of aggregation. Nevertheless, they argued that there was clear value in monitoring trends in risk and protective factors at the population level and, in particular, those factors which were amenable to change.

One factor which emerged clearly as being relevant to self-inflicted death was gender. Over the period studied the rates for men were reported to be around four times those seen in women in England and Wales (Charlton et al, 1992a; 1992b). This difference increased as the rates for men went up while those for women went down. In practice, though, the authors note that it was easier to identify the factors which may have elevated the level of risk for men, than those which were protective for women.

Charlton et al (1992b) went on to analyse the suicide data for England and Wales by occupation, social class and unemployment status. In order to allow comparisons, they calculated the rates in terms of Proportional Mortality Ratio (PMR). This is a method used in epidemiology to calculate the impact of diseases on an exposed population. It is calculated by dividing the number of observed deaths by the number of expected deaths and multiplying by 100. Expected deaths are calculated by applying the total number of suicide deaths in each group in comparison to the number of deaths from suicide in the general population. So, for example, a PMR of 200 for Group A means that group is twice as likely to die from suicide as the general population.

The three occupational groups with the highest rates of suicide were veterinarians, pharmacists and dental surgeons, with PMR's of 364, 217 and 204 respectively. PMRs data though needs to be interpreted with a degree of caution. Increased PMRs for suicide may simply be a result of lower levels of death from other causes. Thus, it could be argued that veterinary surgeons are relatively affluent and may be less likely to die from accidents, injuries, coronary heart disease and so on. This argument though would have less force when looking at farmers, where industrial injury and disease is common yet the PMR is elevated.

It is possible to develop many post-hoc explanations for those groups with elevated PMRs of varying plausibility. A common factor though across vets, pharmacists, medical practitioners is easy access to the means of suicide, including toxic doses of drugs. These groups also more easily cross the threshold for a death by overdose to be defined as suicidal rather than accidental, on the basis that they would understand the effects of drugs on the body and would be unlikely to be unintentionally over-dosing. In contrast, less technically qualified individuals may be given the benefit of doubt. The elevated PMRs seen in groups such as farmers also seems likely to be linked to the availability of means of suicide, with relatively easy access to toxic chemicals and firearms.

Several other potential contributory factors have been suggested. For example, a study into suicide in farmers in the UK (Hawton, 1989) reported a number of contributory factors to be present. These included social isolation, financial pressure and routine access to firearms.

Social class

Charlton et al (1992b) analysed deaths in terms of the Registrar General's classification of socio-economic groups. This is a classification used within the UK to yield broad socio-economic groupings, considering factors such as education and employment status. The classification goes from I (the highest) which includes professional occupations such as physicians, barristers and so on to V (the lowest) which would include groups such as unskilled labourers. The classification would also include the unemployed and a separate group of those whose employment is inadequately described.

Based on this classification, between 1971–85 men in Social Classes II and III had lower than expected Standardised Mortality Ratios (SMRs). Men in Social Class I showed slightly elevated SMRs of 110, whilst men in Social Class V had the highest SMR for suicide at 127. Striking though those recorded on census data as 'unoccupied' and 'inadequately described' showed by far the highest rates. Here the SMRs were 168 and 304 respectively. The latter group were described by the Registrar General as being unemployed, not fully employed, or working outside the mainstream economy. Taken together these groups were at greatly increased risk of suicide and undetermined death.

This finding replicated earlier work (Fox and Shewry, 1988) concerning suicide deaths amongst the unemployed. That study had looked at the years following the 1971 and 1981 national censuses in the UK. In both periods the researchers noted that some of the observed excess mortality could be explained primarily in terms of socio-economic factors, such as unemployment, underemployment and financial hardship. There was also a suggested link to the pattern of SMRs for other causes of death after the 1981 Census such as other s, lung cancer and ischaemic heart disease. An earlier study by Moser et al (1984) also reported a significant increase in risk of self-inflicted deaths in 1971 for men aged 15–64 who were seeking work and their wives.

Many researchers have noted that unemployment is itself a rather crude measure. It identifies the net figures for those unemployed at a given point in time. It also does not serve to determine the negative impact of unemployment. This is liable to be heavily dependent on other factors, including such things as the likelihood of being re-employed and the economic impact of a lack of work.

Some researchers have suggested that the impact of unemployment may be less severe at times of mass unemployment, than at times of low unemployment. Research undertaken by Crombie (1989; 1990) for example, reported no clear correlation between unemployment and suicide levels in Scotland. It is again possible to generate many post hoc explanations for such findings. Such research does though raise several methodological issues. As noted the level of unemployment is a crude measure and its impacts are likely to be different for various groups. It seems questionable whether any relationship between unemployment and suicide could be identified using simple correlations. Indeed Charlton et al (1992b) note that if there is a relationship between unemployment and suicide, it is that is likely to be time lagged, meaning that the relationship would be a complicated one where negative effects emerged later.

Marital status

An analysis of the effects of marital status was conducted by Charlton et al (1992b). The highest rates of suicide were reported to be amongst divorced and widowed men. Widowed men showed higher rates than divorced men in each age groups studied. For all the age groups except those aged 15–24, single, divorced and widowed men had a suicide rate around three times higher than that for married men. Two alternative explanations of this are suggested. It is suggested that marriage may provide some form of protective effect. Alternatively, it may be that men who are more at risk of suicide may be less likely to marry or get divorced at a given age than other men. For women, suicide rates declined across all marital status groups. It would therefore appear that the possible risk and protective factors associated with marital status do not operate in the same way for women. A noteworthy point though is that the Registrar General's figures used do not record cohabitation as a marital status. This has been a growing trend within the UK and the effects of this have not been adequately studied.

Alcohol and drug abuse

A relationship between substance use and suicide has long been recognised within the evidence base. For example, a study conducted by Adelstein and White (1976) looked at a cohort of over 2,000 patients with a history of 'alcoholism'. They found significantly raised suicide levels in men (SMR=320) and women (SMR=230). The risk of suicide amongst those using other drugs has been reported as being much higher than in the general population. Studies have suggested a suicide rate amongst those identified as 'addicts' of around 20 times that seen in the general population (Hawton, 1987). As with studies of marital status though, such correlational research does not tell us the causal mechanism. It is possible that those who use alcohol and other drugs to excess are already at elevated risk of suicide.

Mental Disorder

The two most studied forms of mental disorder in the context of suicide risk, have been schizophrenia and depression. Research has suggested that between ten to 15 per cent of people with a diagnosis of schizophrenia, and 15 per cent of people with a diagnosis of severe depression, went on to kill themselves (Hawton, 1992). An increasing shift away from institutional care for those with mental health problems and the growth of community-based models of care may also impact. Such changes may have had a marked effect of suicide, especially where good risk assessment and management practices are not in place.

Later Research

Kelly and Bunting (1998) reported a study into trends in suicide in England and Wales which built on previous work. It began by addressing definitional issues. The study adopted operational definitions corresponding to ICD codes E950–9 and E980–989 (excluding E988.8), from the International Classification of Diseases 9th revision (ICD-9). They excluded the code E988.8 as since 1979, for England and Wales, it had often been used to accelerate the death registration in the case where a Coroner adjourns an inquest. Nearly all these cases that were resolved turned out to be cases of homicide. It was therefore felt that inclusion of such cases would distort the findings.

For their analysis of those over 15 years at time of death, the authors adopted the broader definition of suicide used by Charlton et al(1992a). However, in their analysis of deaths by gender, and during 'teenage' years, they provided analyses using broad and narrow definitions. The age standardisation in the study was based on the European standard population aged 15 and over.

Gender

In 1982 suicides in men accounted for 63 per cent of all suicides but by 1996 this had increased to 75 per cent. Allowing for changes in the age structure of the population, the standardised rate for men went from 191 per million in 1982 to 174 per million in 1996, a reduction of nine per cent. The rate for men in fact peaked in 1988, at 207 per million. For women, the age standardised rates fell steadily during the period under study, from 98 per million in 1982, to 56 per million in 1996. This represented an overall decrease of 43 per cent. The trends for the broad and narrow legal definitions were similar for both men and women.

Age

The authors tested for a continuation in age related trends by calculating three year moving averages, based on 10-year age groups. For the 3 years centred on 1983, the highest suicide rates were for men aged over 45. Between 1983–1995 though, the suicide rate for men decreased by between 30 and 40 per cent in the 55–64, 65–74 and 75–84 age groups. The rates for the 45–54 group fell less but still reduced by 15 per cent. In contrast the rates for men aged 25–34 rose steadily, from 177 per million in 1983, to 230 per million in 1995, representing an increase of around 30 per cent. This age group also showed the highest overall suicide rate, except for the 85+ age group.

The suicide rates in other age groups showed a differing pattern. For the 15–24 and 35–44 age groups, the rates increased from 1983 to peak in 1991, going on to fall around 10 per cent for both groups by 1995.

For women, a decline in rates was seen across all age groups except for the 15–24 group. The falls in the older age group were marked and were between 45 per cent and 60 per cent for the over 45 age groups. The reduction for younger women aged 35–44 was less marked but was still 27 per cent. In the 25–34 group a small reduction of nine per cent was seen. In contrast though the youngest group (15–24) showed an increase of 16 per cent. It is worth noting that this increase was from a low baseline and despite the increase this group still had by far the lowest rate of suicide, at 35 per million in 1995.

Teenage suicides

Kelly and Bunting analysed suicides in the under 20 years' group in detail. For those aged ten to 19 a greater proportion of deaths were categorised as undetermined rather than suicide by coroner's courts. They did not report any clear trends over the time of the study. As with older age groups though boys appeared at much greater risk than girls. From 1982–96 the researchers noted that there were 2,196 for boys and 684 for girls. There was also a very clear skew towards the older age groups, with suicide amongst pre-pubescents being very rare.

Access and methods

Based on three year moving averages the researchers looked at the four most common methods of suicide. Poisoning (ICD-9 E950–80) was the most common method for women and had become the third most common method for men. The method accounted for around half the total deaths of women and one fifth of those for men. During the period under study though, the use of this method had decreased. A 39 per cent reduction was seen for women and nine per cent reduction for men. Men in the 15–44 age group showed the lowest rates for this method. Overall 55 per cent of such deaths received a suicide verdict, whilst 45 per cent received open verdicts.

The authors noted that there have been suggestions that changes in prescribing practices may have contributed to the decline in this method. In particular, the decreased use of barbiturates and the parallel increase in the use of less toxic benzodiazepines has been reflected in the drugs used in overdoses. The proportion of deaths from analgesics, antipyretics and antirhematics (including paracetamol) remained constant throughout the period studied.

Poisoning by gases and vapours

The number of deaths from poisoning by domestic gas reduced to less than ten per annum, but poisoning by other gases was the second most common method for men, and third most common for women. In 1995 this accounted for 22 per cent of deaths in men and 8 per cent in women.

Use of this method increased for men and women between 1983 and 1991 and then went on to decline until 1995. By 1995 the use of this method had reduced by around a third for both sexes. Such deaths primarily result from carbon monoxide (CO) poisoning from vehicle exhaust gases. The method was far more common in the under 65 age groups, perhaps reflecting access to motor vehicles. The method was also highly likely to be recorded as suicide by coroner's courts (90 per cent). The decline in use in the early-1990s was followed by a dramatic fall in

1993. This change seems most likely to be due to changes in coroner's reporting practices introduced in England and Wales in May 1993. This view receives support from the finding that only this method showed a dramatic fall after May 1993.

The long-term fall in use may also, relate to the mandatory introduction of catalytic converters on new petrol driven cars and vans, from January 1993. Vehicles fitted with these emit much lower levels of toxic gases. In addition, the growth in the use of diesel cars has also been suggested as a factor, since these emit much lower levels of carbon monoxide.

Hanging and suffocation

This was the most common method used by men and in 1995 accounting for around a third of deaths. This compared to around a quarter in 1983. Suicide rates from this method increased steadily over the period 1983–1995. This increase was due entirely to an increase in use of this method in the 15–44 age groups. The rates for all other groups showed a decline.

For women, this was the second most common method used, accounting for around one fifth of deaths in 1995. The use of this method by women has been declining since 1983, but has tended to be used relatively more by younger age groups. Between 1982 and 1984 women used hanging in 49 per cent of cases and suffocation by plastic bag in 37 per cent. Men used hanging in 85 per cent of cases and suffocation by plastic bag in 9 per cent. This had changed for the period 1994–6, with 91 per cent of men choosing hanging and three per cent suffocation. The pattern for women also changed with a marked reduction in the use of this form of suffocation to 20 per cent and an increase in the use of hanging to 68 per cent. Around 90 per cent of such deaths received suicide verdicts at coroner's court.

Drowning

This was the fourth most common method for both men and women. It accounted for nine per cent and 13 per cent of deaths for men and women respectively in 1982. By 1995 this had changed to five per cent and seven per cent respectively. Most deaths were not recorded as suicide by coroners courts, with around 70 per cent receiving 'open' verdicts.

Occupation

Suicide data for two time periods 1982–7 and 1991–6 was assessed, looking at Proportional Mortality Ratios (PMRs) for men and women, by occupation. The researchers analysed men in the 20–64 years' age range and women in the 20–59 age range, including groups which had more than 20 deaths (for men) and 10 deaths (for women). In addition, they included groups which had shown high PMRs in previous studies, even where the number of deaths was lower than these thresholds (e.g. veterinarians).

For the period 1982–87 veterinarians showed the highest PMR at 349, followed by farmers and librarians at 202 and 226 respectively. By 1991–6 vets and farmers were second and third, but had been overtaken by dentists with a PMR of 249. For all but one of the occupational groups with significantly high PMRs there was a decrease between the earlier and latter periods. Librarians showed the largest decrease of 63 per cent. The only occupation to show an increase (30 per cent) were dentists.

For women, medical practitioners, therapists and pharmacists showed the highest PMRs in the earlier period (355, 269 and 274 respectively). In the later period, medical practitioners, domestic housekeepers and veterinarians showed the highest levels (285, 247 and 500 respectively). Women classified as students also had significantly higher PMRs at 144 and 139 over the two-time periods. However, the researchers noted that PMRs show the likelihood that a death in a given occupation is from suicide rather than another cause. Students tend to be younger and the likelihood of them dying from any cause is very low.

In both time periods occupations from Social Classes I and II predominated. The researchers suggested that this was largely an artefact of the way PMR's are calculated. Men in Social Classes I and II had much lower *rates* of suicide than men in Social Class V. The high PMRs found for in younger cohorts of doctors, vets and dentists reflected in large part the low overall mortality making the proportion of deaths from suicide high, relative to other causes.

The authors also note an apparent trend for professions with high PMRs to be from medical or related types of profession, rather than law or accountancy. This led them to suggest that ease of access and knowledge about drugs and other methods of suicide were a key factor.

Marital status

The authors reported that the rates for women in all marital status groups declined over the period of the study, except for those who were single. In this respect the pattern for women had become more like that traditionally reported for men. Kelly and Bunting suggest that this finding is likely to be of increasing significance, since current population trends show increasing numbers of women living alone. They went on to suggest that single women tended to live alone more often, and as such may have lost important sources of emotional support.

Previous studies have suggested that single or divorced men are at greater risk of suicide than married men. This was confirmed for the period under study.

drug and alcohol misuse

Deaths rates from alcohol related causes of death were reported to have continued to rise over the period studied. This was true for both men and women in the 15–44 years and 45+ year's groups, although with much higher rates seen for men. This trend continued, despite the observed reductions in the suicide rate.

Deaths related to drug abuse increased for the 15–44 years' group, with men four times more likely to die from such causes (ICD9 codes 304 and 305.2–9). This led the researchers to suggest revisions to early notions that increases in drug and alcohol abuse were major factors in increasing the suicide rate. If an association exists, they suggested that it is not as straightforward as was initially suggested and may be moderated by factors such as gender.

Comparative Research

Comparison of trends in suicide across different countries presents a few challenges in terms of interpretation. Where clear commonalities are found internationally in terms of data collection, they are though likely to be a more reliable estimate of changes in suicide.

In the work by Charlton et al(1992a; 1992b) it is noted that within the UK, Scotland and Northern Ireland showed higher suicide rates than England and Wales. The trends for men in the 25–44 age group appeared to differ across Western countries. There was a notable decline in the rates of suicide for West Germany, whilst in the United States the rates appeared to remain level. In France, even more marked increases were seen than in the UK.

Across Western countries the trends for women appeared generally like those for men. The two exceptions to this have been the UK and USA, where the trends for men and women have gone in opposite directions. The risk for men has overall gone up and the risk for women down.

Neeleman, Mak and Wesseley (1997) reported the results of a three-year (1991–1993) survey of unnatural deaths in an inner London area. They compared 'true likely' and 'official' suicide rates. The analysis included 553 deaths that had been recorded at the local coroner's court and were defined as being attributable to unnatural causes (i.e. suicide, open, accidental and drug dependency verdicts).

They went on to report age standardised mortality ratios (SMRs) by ethnicity, using the 'white' group as the standard for comparison. The authors combined 'black Caribbean' and 'black other' groups and used the method described by Van Os et al(1996) to correct for census under-enumeration amongst African-Caribbean men in the UK. A total of 20 cases in the sample had not received official suicide verdicts. The odds of a non-suicide verdict were reported to be higher in deaths of women compared with men with odds ratio (OR) of 2.2. Deaths resulting from passive methods such as suffocation were also more likely to be recorded as suicides compared with other methods with an OR of 6.4. Deaths of those from ethnic minority groups were more likely to be seen as suicides with an OR of 2.1 and this also applied to whites not born in England and Wales compared with those who were born there with an OR of 2.5.

The authors reported that Afro-Caribbean men and especially women had lower age standardised suicide rates than whites. Women born on the Indian sub-continent though were reported to have higher SMRs than white women. The authors also identified a trend amongst young African-Caribbean men with increased rates, like those seen in young white men.

In discussing their results Neeleman et al raised several points. Firstly they noted that they replicated the finding that official suicide rate substantially underestimated the likely true frequency of suicide. They also suggest that there was a high rate of suicide observed, by international standards. Secondly, they note that the SMRs for African-Caribbean's was lower than for whites, with the exception of young African-Caribbean men, who appeared to have rates similar to young white men. They found the SMRs for Indian and Asian women to be higher than the SMR for white women. Thirdly they noted that in contrast to other research (Charlton, 1995; Obafunwa and Busuttil, 1994) young white men showed higher suicide rates than older age groups.

Overall a number of trends observed in suicide in the community within the UK, have been reflected in international studies. The rate of suicide for men has remained higher than that for women, a finding which has been widely replicated in the UK, Europe and North America.

Several broad trends in suicide have been described in the UK. These have included the effects of war and economic dislocation. During the first and second world wars marked decreases were observed, with a marked increase during the inter-war period of economic depression. Such findings appear to have been present in other developed economies experiencing these events.

After World War II, suicides for men and women rose to a peak in 1963, with the increase for women being proportionally greater than that for men. After 1963 the rates of suicide for men and women began to decline. This continued for women but for men the rate began to rise again from the 1970s onwards. The rate for suicides and undetermined deaths rose in parallel during the same period. This was the first time since 1911 that suicide trends for men and women had moved in opposite directions.

Broad changes in the methods of suicide have also been observed, often because of social changes. Domestic gas poisoning went from being one of the most common methods of self-inflicted death in the community to being very rare. It was largely replaced, especially amongst younger age groups and men, with poisoning due to motor vehicle exhaust gas. This paralleled the wider availability of motor vehicles internationally.

Researchers have suggested many factors associated with suicide and undetermined deaths. These have included illness (both mental and physical). Personal factors such as social support and attitudes to suicide. Occurrence of stressful life events. Changes in the wider cultural and economic environment. And finally access to means of completing suicide. Research into such factors and the interactions between them remains in its infancy.

One marked finding has been role of unemployment in suicide. This has been shown to result in excess mortality over and above that due to adverse socio-economic factors. Such excess mortality has been observed in men aged 15–64 who were seeking work and also in their wives.

Amongst women in the UK the suicide rate declined across all marital status groupings from 1911 until the early-1990s. For men, being single or divorced was associated with increased risk of suicide. It was therefore suggested that the possible risk and protective factors associated with marital status did not operate in the same way for women as for men. More recently though single women in younger age groups have shown a pattern of increased risk of suicide similar to that seen in men. To date the social changes in marriage and cohabiting have received little research attention, and remain very poorly understood.

In 1982 suicides in men accounted for 63 per cent of all suicides. By 1996 this had increased to 75 per cent. Allowing for changes in the age structure of the population, the standardised rate of suicide for men reduced by nine per cent. The rate of suicide for men in the UK reached a peak in 1988, at 20.7 per 100,000. For women the age standardised rates have fallen steadily, to a rate of 5.6 per 100,000 in 1996.

Recent Trends

A study by Mok et al (2012) compared Scotland with other nations of the UK over the period from 1960 to 2008. The researchers used operational definitions of suicide and self-inflicted deaths based on ICD codes, drawing on the 9th and 10th revisions of this framework.

The researchers noted that the trends seen in Scotland diverged from those seen in other parts of the UK over time. They suggested that three clear periods were observed: 1960–1967, 1968–1991 and 1992–2008. For the period 1961–67 they noted a decline in the rates for males across the

UK, with a decline in Scotland that was not statistically significant. A similar pattern was observed for women.

The second time period (1968–91) showed a marked increase in rates of suicide across the UK for men. The increase in Scotland was significantly greater than that seen in England and Wales. In common with the UK as a whole the rates of female suicides in Scotland fell over this time period.

Within the third time period (1992–2008) the researchers suggest a marked divergence of Scotland from the pattern seen in the rest of the UK. Here rates in Scotland increased while those in England and Wales decreased. This difference appeared to be primarily due to increased death rates in younger men (15–34), with a small increase in young women in Scotland (Mok et al, 2012).

A study by Barr et al (2012) looked at the effects a marked economic change in the UK by analysing the effects on suicide of the financial crisis of 2007–2008. In assessing this the researchers looked at the predicted rate of suicide and compared this to the observed rate between 2008 and 2010. Based on historic trends they reported an excess of 846 suicides in men and 155 in women during this period. They went on to suggest that a 10 per cent increase in the number of unemployed men was significantly associated with a 1.4 per cent increase in male suicides.

Subsequently the long-term trends appear to have resumed as high rates of unemployment did not follow from 2008. In 2014, there were 6,122 suicides in the UK, representing a two per cent (120) reduction over the 2013 figures. The overall rate had reduced to 10.8 deaths per 100,000 of population with reductions for both men and women. The male rate of suicide though remained three times higher than that for women, with 16.8 men per 100,000 of population dying in this manner, compared to 5.2 per 100,000 women. The highest rate of suicides was seen in men aged from 45 to 59, with 23.9 completed suicides per 100,000.

Comparisons across the UK suggested a continued divergence of Scotland and Northern Ireland compared to England and Wales. Scotland showed higher rate of suicides at 14.5 deaths per 100,000 of population, compared to 10.3 in England and 9.2 in Wales. Northern Ireland showed the highest rate at 16.5 deaths per 100,000. Marked regional variations were also evidence with the North of England showing the highest rate in England (13.2) compared to the lowest in London (7.8).

Conclusions *Chapter 3*

Most recent studies into suicide in the community have drawn on operational definitions of suicide, rather than on legally derived verdicts. Such definitions have, most frequently, drawn on World Health Organization definitions of causes of deaths. These have two major advantages in respect of suicide research: (i) they have enabled comparisons to be made directly between different studies; (ii) they have avoided excluding large numbers of self-inflicted deaths on a largely arbitrary basis from the research. The use of legal definitions of suicide has fortunately all but ceased in community studies. The use of broader operational definitions of suicide (e.g. Hawton, Comabella, Haw, C. et.al., 2013; Appleby, Kapur, Shaw, et.al. 2015) have been employed allowing international comparisons.

Several consistent findings have emerged from the community research base, with several factors being consistently associated with an increased risk of suicide in the UK. Many of these have also been seen internationally.

A clear and enduring risk factor has been gender, with men being shown to be at consistently significantly greater risk of suicide. As a risk factor the contribution is large with men typically showing rates around three times those for women.

Age also tends to emerge as a factor in suicide in the community, although here the association is complicated. Rates of suicide in younger groups have often appeared to be inflated, because of low mortality from other causes.

Health factors have consistently emerged as important. This applies to both physical and mental health. Serious physical illnesses show an association with self-inflicted deaths. So too does the occurrence of serious mental health issues, with elevated rates for those suffering serious disorders such as psychosis or depression. In addition, those who have problems with drug use (including alcohol) appear to be at increased risk. Those with a history of non-lethal self-injury also present a markedly increased risk of subsequent suicide (Hawton, Saunders and O'Connor 2012). Notions that those who self-injure are not at genuine risk of suicide appear to be entirely misplaced.

Studies have consistently suggested that some occupational groups may be at markedly higher risk of suicide. Such studies have often been based on the calculation of Proportional Mortality Ratios (PMRs), and have suggested that some professional groups were at increased risk of suicide. Later research has, to a significant degree, called this into question, suggesting that much of the effect may simply be an artefact of the way such statistics are calculated. This is supported by the findings that professional groups have much lower rates of suicide. A more robust finding has been that those in unskilled occupations show the highest rates of suicide amongst employed groups.

A further consistent finding has been that those who are unemployed, or in inadequately defined forms of employment outside the mainstream economy, have the highest rates of suicide. Levels of suicide in these groups have generally been higher than for any employed groups. In addition, periods of high unemployment have often been associated with later increases in the rates of suicide in a time-lagged manner. The association between unemployment and suicide does not appear to be a simple one and may operate through its effects on mental health in general and depression in particular.

As noted at the start of this chapter, findings from the community are critical to understanding suicide in prisons. Prisons do not operate in vacuum and they will typically show much higher levels of the risk factors identified in the community. Prisons will contain disproportionate numbers of the unemployed. They also show much higher levels of those with mental health problems. Because of the often-inadequate implementation of community mental health care, prisons have often become placements of last resort for those who would, in the past, have been in hospitals. In addition, all prisons will contain disproportionate numbers of those with alcohol and drug abuse. This suggests that any comparisons between prisons and the community need to be treated with circumspection.

CHAPTER 4

What We Know About Prisoners

Introduction

In 2002 the UK Government produced a report entitled *Reducing Re-Offending by Ex-prisoners*. The report, which was published in July of that year was commissioned because of well-established concerns that the rates of re-offending by ex-prisoners were consistently and unacceptably high. It took as its starting point a detailed review of who ended up in prison. Nine key areas were reviewed which it was felt linked to persistent offending. These were:

family networks

   I.   Institutionalisation and life-skills

  II.   Education and training

 III.   Employment

 IV.   Drug and alcohol misuse

  V.   Mental and physical health

 VI.   Attitudes and self-control

 VII.   Housing

VIII.   Financial support and debt

These areas can be taken as capturing the range of experiences a person has had over the course of their lives. The divisions are of course arbitrary. The areas will both overlap and interact. For example, educational experiences are likely to depend on attitudes but also on developmental background and family circumstances. The categories used by the Social Exclusion Unit have been used as a framework below but with the proviso that this is for descriptive purposes, rather than suggesting clear distinctions.

Family, Attitudes and Self-Control

Early experience

There is an extensive evidence base that demonstrates the profound effects of early experience, as well as the long term psychological and social consequences. Poor developmental environments have been repeatedly shown to have long-term adverse consequences for many of those who experience then. These include poorer educational outcomes, health outcomes as well as more delinquent and criminal behaviour. This is not to suggest this is a deterministic process. Nor is it exclusively a matter of material wealth. Some children and families show remarkable levels of resilience in the face of adversity. Children born into materially poor environments can do well, typically where their environment is enriched in other ways. It is to suggest that, at a population level, the effects will be negative (e.g. Rutter and Taylor, 2005; Skeels and Dye, 1947).

The psychological and social effects from developmental experiences may be subtle and not involve abuse or severe neglect. This is illustrated by the extensive work on attachment in children and adults and the effects of this on later behaviour and attitudes towards others. The process of bonding with and becoming attached to others seems to take place very early in development. It also seems to have major impacts on later development, across a range of domains. It is a process that has been extensively researched.

Attachment to others has been observed to take place in humans and other species. It seems to do so very early and has been seen within 6–12 hours after birth. It can though take place much later than this. What appear to be evident is that the process normally takes place within a critical period in childhood. Where this fails, attachment becomes much harder to achieve (Harlow and Harlow, 1965; Rutter and Taylor, 2005).

Attachment has also been observed to be a reciprocal process, involving both the temperament of the children and those around them. Early research in this area described systematic differences in new born children

(Thomas and Chess, 1996). These were described as falling along three major dimensions:

1. Reactive or negative emotion.
2. Self-regulation.
3. Approach/withdrawal, inhibition.

Early thinking in this area suggested that these differences were largely inherent in the child, resulting largely from genetic variation along with some in utero effects (Thomas and Chess, 1996). Later research suggested a rather more complex process than this, with differences relating much more to the characteristics of the dyadic interactions between the child and its main caregivers. These characteristics appeared to largely reflect the caregivers understanding of the child. Thus, transactional models are currently favoured in this area, where initial characteristics or perceptions may become reinforced and amplified over time because of patterns of care. The long-term effects associated with these early relationships may be marked.

Processes of attachment and resilience have been subject to extensive study since the early work in this area. This has drawn on observational studies and experimental studies that have manipulated separation and return of attachment figures to assess the impacts of these (Ainsworth et al, 1978). The evidence from such studies led to initial suggestions that four primary types of attachment relationship could be described. It was suggested that these were:

A. Avoidant: Here the child tends to show conspicuous avoidance when reunited. They may not be distressed at all during separation and any distress shown seems to be related to being left alone, rather than the absence of the attachment figure.

B. Secure: Here the child will actively seek to maintain contact and proximity especially when reunited. Such children may show distress when separated and this appears linked to the attachment figures absence.

C. Ambivalent: This group of children tend to show a pattern of contact and interaction with resistance. For example, wanting to be picked up then pushing away the attachment figure.

D.   Disorganised: This group was a later addition and children here tend to show no clear pattern of behaviour, often showing bizarre and disrupted patterns of behaviour on reunion (Ainsworth, Blehar, Waters and Wall, 1978).

Later research has increasingly moved away from the notion that attachment happens in early life. More recent work has noted that it may be a lifelong process and that problems with attachment may occur throughout a person's life. More positive views in this area have derived in part from studies of children and adults who show marked resilience and capacity to recover from poor early circumstances. Attachment appears to become increasingly internalised with increasing age. Individuals with a history of secure attachment appear as a group to have better outcomes, with better mental health and lower rates of delinquent behaviours. Those with insecure or ambivalent attachments have a more negative outlook (Crittenden and Claussen, 2003; Crittenden, 2015).

Several attempts have been made to study attachment effects in older children and adults. One study of eight to 12 year olds being treated for behavioural problems compared their patterns of attachment to a control group. The group showing behavioural problems showed significant differences from those children not receiving intervention work. They tended to show more insecure and ambivalent attachment patterns to others. The insecurely attached children also tended to deny being anxious about separation or they gave what were described by the researchers as inappropriate or bizarre responses (Wright, Binney and Smith, 1995).

Several studies have been undertaken to look at continuity in attachment over time. The current evidence suggests a high degree of continuity but also the possibility of marked discontinuities. Importantly shifts from secure to insecure attachment have been seen in children. These appeared to be clearly linked to social factors and shifts towards insecure attachment were generally associated with mothers reporting negative life events. Shifts from insecure to secure attachment tended to be associated with positive life events (Vaughan Egeland, Sroufe and Waters, 1979).

A later study (Fonagy, Steele, Steele et al, 1994) looked at a sample of 100 mothers and 100 fathers, who were followed up over time. The researchers went on to look at the impacts of disrupted parenting and deprivation on the children. Evidence of ongoing negative effects was reported but this was also mediated by the way negative experiences were dealt with. The researchers went on to identify a group of children who showed marked resilience and they termed these 'earned secures'. This referred to those children who had marked negative childhood experiences but had shown resilience to and the ability to overcome these experiences. The researchers suggested that this seemed to be primarily the result of cognitive processes of reflection and analysis. These children seemed able to understand their own negative experiences and alter their attitudes and behaviour to offset the negative effects. The group contrasted with the group of children who had shown continuously (unearned) secure attachment, linked to continuous positive experiences. The researchers noted though that both secure groups seemed to have had more experiences of positive parenting than the insecurely attached group. This perhaps suggests that even the 'earned' secure group needed some positive experiences to aid their resilience.

Family relationships

Disrupted family relationships have also been extensively researched and these appear to have significant negative impacts. An example of this is the effects of divorce or relationship breakups. In a study of 144 children, half from divorced families, several negative effects were observed amongst the children in the divorced group. One year post divorce most children reported emotional distress and showed behavioural problems associated with disrupted family relationships and functioning. These behaviour problems were reported to be reduced after two years but there were some notable exceptions to this. Boys appeared to be especially susceptible to ongoing problems, showing poor relationships with mothers who had custody of them. These boys showed increased levels of anti-social and defiant behaviours (Hetherington et al, 1982; Hetherington, 1989). A follow up study conducted after six years found several significant differences between these groups. The children in divorced families had experienced greater independence at an early age than the group whose parents did not divorce. Girls also seemed to fare better than boys. The quality of relationships between mothers and daughters was similar for both groups. In contrast relationships between mothers and sons continued to show difficulties in those families where mothers had not remarried. The family situation prior to divorce appeared to be of marked relevance to the outcomes. For those already dealing with adverse circumstances, divorce tended to make matters significantly worse (Cherlin et al, 1991).

Other forms of family disruption also appear to have significant impacts. For example, a study of the effects of step families looked at a group of children between the ages of six to 16 years. Those who experienced step-families showed an increased risk of drug abuse, juvenile crime and poor school achievement. These effects seemed to be primarily a result of pre-existing family disruption, social and economic deprivation and parent characteristics. Children already experiencing adverse family conditions appeared more likely to experience step parenting and step families (Nicholson, Fergusson and Horwood, 1999).

Adolescence is a period of rapid change and development and has also been associated with an increase in family conflict. For most children, this may have been overstated but for those who have already experienced adversity this may be marked. This small sub-group was characterised by high levels of conflict and for some outright rejection of their parents. This pattern has been reported to be more common in children with prior histories of behavioural (Rutter et al, 1976; Freiberg, Homel and Lamb, 2013).

Child abuse and physical punishment

Correlations between physical punishment, poor behaviour and aggression in children have been extensively reported (Smith, Cowie and Blades, 2004). One review of physical abuse reported a marked association between these experiences in childhood and later criminal offending, adult familial violence and non-familial violence (Malinowski-Rummel and Hansen, 1993). Negative effects have also been reported to be associated with the use of physical punishments during childhood (Fergusson, 2013). Sexual abuse has also been reported to be associated with poorer long-term mental health (Fergusson, McLeod, and Horwood, 2013).

Peer groups

Peers groups have a marked impact from an early age. This initially involves the development of social behaviours, with interactions becoming more sophisticated over time. This typically begins with parallel play where children play similar 'games' alongside each other. Group play also begins early and increases for most children with age.

At around six years of age boys and girls take separate paths and until puberty boys and girls tend to show low levels of interaction with the other gender. Peer activity also differs with boys tending to focus on group activity with structured rules, playing in larger groups and age ranges. Girls tend to focus more on exclusive friendships and smaller group activities (Maccoby, 1998).

Adolescence is associated with marked change. Although same sex groupings remain common there is a re-emergence of social relationships between the genders. Some children though tend to be excluded from social groupings either through rejection or neglect. The most common reason for such rejection is high levels of aggressive behaviour, typically shown by boys. This group also tend to show higher levels of dishonesty, more impulsivity and higher levels of non-co-operation with peers. Rejection of this group appears to be relatively stable over time and is associated with poor academic performance. For older boys, aggression could also be useful in overcoming rejection. Here older boys can assert higher social status and so join in peer activities, although this does not appear to be the case for boys showing very high levels of aggression (Sandstrom and Coie, 1999).

Aggression

The small group who show very high levels of aggression are significantly more likely to show later delinquent and criminal behaviour (Farrington, 1995). Such aggression is correlated with poor home circumstances, and particularly a lack of parental warmth, poor parental monitoring of activities and ineffective discipline at home (Patterson et al, 1989). This group also show higher levels of academic failure and peer rejection. During adolescence, they are more likely to be drawn to anti-social peer groups which may, in turn, play an important role in the development of delinquent and criminal behaviour (Farrington, 2015a; 2015b). Such children tend to form anti-social peer groups which may result in escalation of behaviour (Berndt and Keefe, 1995).

During adolescence levels of anti-social and criminal behaviour increases rapidly to a peak in the later teenage years. Longitudinal studies suggest several effective predictors of this. At the age of 8 hyperactivity, impulsivity, difficulty with attention, marital discord, harsh or erratic parenting and socioeconomic deprivation predict later criminal behaviours (Farrington and West, 1990; Farrington, Loeber and VanKamen, 1990; Shepherd and Farrington, 1995; Farrington, 2015a; 2015b). Studies looking at resilience and desistance have suggested that these areas may act cumulatively and synergistically (Farrington, 1994; Kazmian and Farrington, 2015). Provision of support and training and good quality preschool education have been shown to reduce these negative effects when they are accurately targeted on children at high risk (Farrington, 1994).

The research in developmental psychology makes clear that those who go on to show and continue delinquent and criminal behaviour have typically had a range of adverse experiences (Farrington, 2015a; 2015b; Kazmian and Farrington, 2015). In turn those who end up imprisoned are a selected sub-sample of this group. It is difficult to over emphasise the importance of the developmental research in this area and the role of these findings in developing services (Towl, 2015). An adequate understanding of suicide in prisons needs to take as it starting point the characteristics of prisoners. It has also been argued that this needs to go beyond approaches based on categories of mental health disorder towards models based on an adequate psychological understanding of needs (Crighton and Towl, 1997).

Attitudes and self-control

The area of attitudes and self-control is highlighted by the Social Exclusion Unit as an area contributing to delinquent and criminal behaviour. It is certainly the case that some prisoners will have negative and anti-social attitudes and behaviour. The fact that these are often obvious may account for the somewhat surprising stress on this area which has come to be a primary focus for work within prisons and to a lesser extent the community. The approach to this has seen the growth of structured group work designed to modify attitudes and improve self-control. Such work is relatively easy to set up, deliver, measure and charge for. It is though largely predicated on an assumption that behavioural change will follow attitude change. This assumption is not well founded and a great deal of psychological research has noted the limitations of such a view. It has been noted that in many respects this reflects attributional biases commonly seen in people. It may reflect a fundamental tendency to locate the causes of others behaviour as being due to their internal characteristics and underestimating the external effects (Nisbett and Ross, 1980).

The extent to which prisoner's attitudes and poor self-control have resulted in their behaviour, as opposed to the conditions they find themselves in, remains contentious (Zimbardo, 2007).

Health

Prisoners as a group are younger than the general population. If they were a random cross section of this younger age range, this would lead to an expectation of relatively good physical health. This assumption is not though correct. Prisoners are drawn from groups that tend to show higher levels of poverty and social exclusion. Not unrelated to this they are also more likely to engage in a range of behaviours that have adverse effects on health. They are more likely to smoke tobacco than those of a similar age who are not imprisoned. They also tend to use more alcohol and more illicit drugs (Marshall, Simpson and Stevens, 2000). They also appear to engage in more high risk sexual behaviours and to be at greater risk of sexually transmitted infections (Curran, McHugh and Nooney, 1989).

Previous research has been undertaken looking at the health of prisoners (e.g. Bridgwood and Malbon, 1995; Herbert, Plugge, Foster and Doll, 2012). These have consistently suggested that prisoners show elevated risk across many areas. For example, prisoners show high levels of tobacco use in prisons, with those in the 18–49 age range being more than twice as likely to be smokers, compared to the general population. Notably smoking in the community has been in decline and has been increasingly restricted in public areas. In prisons, few if any efforts have been made to address this (Towl, 2006). High prevalence of alcohol problems is also seen in prisons with around three out of four prisoners reporting significant problems and around one in three showing possible dependence (MacAskill, Parkes, Brooks et al, 2011).

The role of diet in the health of prisoners has been relatively neglected until recently. Prisoners tend to report a poor diet when in the community, eating less fresh fruit and vegetables and less fatty foods than in prison. They also reported consuming less biscuits and cakes. In this area prisoners appear in the past to have been significantly better fed than similarly aged peers in the community, with lower rates of obesity. Possibly linked to this the blood pressure of prisoners was found to be significantly lower than the general population (Bridgwood and Malbon, 1995).

In health terms prisoners seem to make physical health gains whilst in custody. These appear to be linked to improved diet alng with reduced alcohol and drug use. Prisoners will also typically experience better access to healthcare, although recent changes to primary healthcare in prisons may have reduced this effect. These gains though do not appear to be maintained for many prisoners when they return to the community. The links between the diet of prisoners and behaviour have only recently become the focus of serious research and attention. A review of this area suggested that a range of behavioural problems may be associated with dietary deficiencies in the form of macro-malnutrition (e.g. protein) and micro-malnutrition (e.g. iron and zinc). Such malnutrition was found to have marked adverse effects on behaviour but such effects could be easily reversible, through provision of better diet (Liu and Raine, 2006). Several mechanisms have been suggested for this, involving impairments to neurocognitive functioning. Much of this research has been undertaken in North America, where issues of poor diet may be more marked than in Europe. The trends towards obesity and malnutrition appear though to be following a similar trend in the UK. Such research findings are also of current relevance to prisons, in the context of ongoing trends to reduce the costs of prison to relatively low levels.

Mental health, as compared with physical helath, has been much more of a focus for the prison population. In turn much of this focus has been on the identification of types of mental disorder and the use of these as predictors of criminal re-offending. This approach has been extensively and reasonably criticised on several grounds. Most strikingly the approach can be tautological. Allocating prisoners to categories is used to both describe and account for outcomes. The best that can be said of this is that it is of limited explanatory value. At worst, it risks simply pathologising responses to social and psychological adversity.

The most obvious example of this in prisons has been the concept of personality disorder. Here prisoners are categorised based on the presence of marked attitudes and behaviours. The circularity of the approach when used to explain the behaviour is clear in the case of 'anti-social personality disorder'. Here the disorder is defined by anti-social behaviour and may subsequently be used to 'explain' it.

With such limitations in mind though, the prevalence of mental disorder in prisoners does appear to be higher than in the community. An extensive study in 1997 looked at this for imprisoned men and women (Singleton, et al 1998). Based on a large sample of prisoners the researchers found that over half the men on remand had no educational qualifications. Just over a third indicated that they had been in legal work prior to imprisonment. In terms of the mental disorder prevalence rates 'personality disorder' was common. Using the Diagnostic and Statistical Manual IV (DSM IV) categories 78 per cent of men on remand, 64 per cent of sentenced men and 31 per cent of women prisoners showed evidence of 'personality disorders'. Most commonly identified was 'antisocial personality disorder' at 63 per cent of men on remand), 49 per cent of sentenced men and 31 per cent of women on remand and sentenced.

Those who were categorised in this way tended to share several characteristics. They tended to be younger and perhaps related to this unmarried. They also tended to be white and were more often charged with acquisitive offences.

The authors reported differences in the identification of psychotic experiences (primarily hallucinations and delusional beliefs (Oltmanns and Maher, 1988)) between the clinical and lay interviewers. The rates for such experiences ranged from four per cent to 21 per cent, with sentenced men showing lower rates. Reported rates of such experiences in women on remand were about twice the level seen in men.

Previous 'self-harm' was considered by the researchers using a broad definition. This included previous suicidal ideation, self-injury and suicide attempts. Around two per cent of men on remand reported attempting suicide in the previous week. Remand prisoners also reported slightly higher levels of suicidal ideation and attempts. Higher rates of 'self-harm' were also reported for white prisoners and lower rates for black prisoners. This is consistent with large scale UK based empirical work into prisoner suicides (see for example, Crighton and Towl, 2002).

Histories of alcohol misuse were also relatively common and more so for white prisoners. The rate of alcohol misuse for white remand prisoners was reported to be around double that for black remand prisoners. White prisoners were also more likely to report misuse of opiates and stimulant drugs such as cocaine and amphetamines. Women prisoners held on remand showed very high levels of injecting drug use and 28 per cent reported having injected drugs in the month prior to imprisonment. Around four in ten women reported a history of injecting drugs. Around half of those in the study said they had been dependent on drugs to some degree in the year before coming into custody.

A concerning finding from this research was the poor level of support to drug and alcohol users in prison. A high proportion reported healthcare staff being unwilling to provide help. The proportion reporting that help was unavailable in prison was almost double that in the community. It seems likely that this will have changed significantly since the research was undertaken with significant investment in drugs interventions with prisoners in recent years (Towl, 2006).

As highlighted above those with difficult histories are more likely to be imprisoned and this was reflected in some key findings for this study. One in three women and one in ten imprisoned men reported being sexually abused in childhood. Given the well-documented tendency towards under-reporting this may be an underestimate the actual levels of abuse.

Subsequent research has confirmed this pattern of relatively high levels of a broad range of mental health needs (Humber, Webb, Piper et al, 2013; MacDonald, 2013). This problem has been exacerbated by an apparent professional reluctance to work with this group of people with high levels of need and varying levels of service provision that have little to do with need (Forrester, Exworthy, Olumoroti, et al, 2013).

Education

One consistent finding over time is that men and women who are imprisoned tended to have low levels of educational attainment. It is perhaps salutary to note that this is far from being a recent discovery. A study in the 1920s and 1930s for example, looked at prison education in the United States. This work identified problems in the teaching of basic skills, as well as weaknesses in vocational education in prison (MacCormick, 1931). The author went on to note that prisoners experience of formal education has often not been positive. They went on to advocate the eradication of illiteracy and efforts to deliver education in ways that were relevant to prisoners, including efforts to develop constructive use of leisure time. Such recommendations look strikingly current.

Another key finding has been that education is associated with a reduction in reoffending and this appears to be the case for a very wide range of academic and vocational education (Chappell, 2004; Crighton, 2006, 2008). There has been some suggestion that this only applies to the provision of vocational and basic education. More advanced education, it has been suggested, may simply result in more skilled criminals. This view has influenced recent policy and practice in prisons in England and Wales, with the withdrawal of most funding for all except basic education and vocational work. The basis for this though appears to be founded on largely on prejudice. Current evidence suggests that more advanced and non-vocational education is effective in reducing rates of reconviction (Kim and Clark, 2013).

Housing

As with education the association between housing and crime is long established. Those who lack accommodation are at greater risk of imprisonment, as are those who lack secure accommodation. The relevance of this has been highlighted in recent work in the UK (Williams, Poyser and Hopkins, 2012). This study found high levels of homelessness prior to custody at 15 per cent of prisoners. They contrasted this with the fact that around 3.5 per cent of the general population reported ever having been homeless. Even those who were not homeless faced problems with accommodation and many reported being in short term accommodation, with 28 per cent living in their accommodation for less than six months.

A large proportion also said that they would face problems when released, with 37 per cent saying they would need help finding a place to live. Of this group 84 per cent anticipated serious difficulty saying they would need a lot of help. Those with previous sentences including probation and community orders were more likely to report needing help finding accommodation and were more likely to have been homeless before entering prison. Such difficulties were linked to other needs and those with a history of drug or alcohol abuse were more likely to report needing help with accommodation.

Income

The evidence in this area is both clear and long established. Prisoners are drawn disproportionately from the poorest members of society. There is also a cycle of disadvantage, with the children and families of prisoners being more likely to be under financial stress and more likely to go on to be imprisoned (Social Exclusion Unit, 2002). Low relative incomes are also associated with a range of other adverse effects. As a group, poorer members of society often suffer from poorer and less secure housing, poorer mental health and greater levels of debt (Jenkins, Bhugra, Bebbington et al, 2008).

In this area, recent policy changes, as well as long-term economic trends in the UK, seem likely to have made this worse. Following the banking collapse of 2008 state support of various kinds was progressively reduced and this is likely to hit poorer groups harder, as they are more dependent on this provision than wealthier groups. They are, as a group, also less likely to have other forms of 'social capital' on which they can draw. For prisons, this is likely to mean that prisoners arrive with increased experience of financial and associated hardships (Crewe, 2012).

Conclusions *Chapter 4*

The review of prisoner characteristics outlinedin this chapter suggests several themes. Prisoners are very clearly not a random cross-section of the general population. They are drawn selectively from the wider community, as the result of social processes. Many factors act to increase the risk of delinquent and criminal behaviour and these have been subject to extensive research. Additionally, there are biases that act within the Criminal Justice System, that will further select those who are imprisoned rather than being subject to other forms of punishment.

The result of these processes is that prisons will disproportionality receive the most disadvantaged and poorest members of society. They will tend to receive those with poorer physical and mental health, often from insecure accommodation or homelessness. They will tend to be those who have had the most difficult starts in life and they may have had poor or no family support. Many will have been victims of crime as well as perpetrators. In relation to suicide this is a listing of many of the risk factors that have been identified for suicide and self-injury, which perhaps illustrates the enormous scale of the challenge facing prisons. It also perhaps goes, at least some way, to explaining the elevated levels of suicide seen in prison.

CHAPTER 5

The Management of Suicide in Prisons

Introduction

One of the key distinctions helpfully highlighted in the Harris Review into prisoner suicide was the evident mismatch between Prison Service policies and sometimes practices. On the whole, the policies were viewed positively through the lens of the that review. But there were concerns around the enactment of policies in prisons (Harris Review, 2015). Since the Harris Review, there is probably good cause to be even more concerned about this mismatch between anticipated plans and delivery. This is because records of violence in prisons are on the increase. Members of the Prison Officers Association (POA) have had planned walk outs of some prisons because, they have said, of concerns about staff safety and a desire to help secure a meeting with the Home Secretary.

One structural problem for senior leaders in HM Prison Service is that with the further marketisation of prisons and services in prisons in the 21st-Century, this makes for a more complex operating environment in organizing or ensuring the delivery of a coherent suicide prevention policy in prisons. This challenge is evident in the relevant instruction to prison leaders on the management of prisoners at an inflated risk of harm to themselves and to and from others, as it is put in the official documentation (Ministry of Justice, 2011). The latter reference appears to be to bullying but it is perhaps noteworthy that this is a term which does not seem to be being used in official accounts of prisons, again something picked up in the Harris Review. The processes and procedures associated with the management of the suicidal are in general subject to continued comment and dialogue with the Independent Advisory Panel (IAP) on

Deaths in Custody having been informed of further work in this vital area. There can sometimes appear to be a defensiveness on the part of prison officials struggling to run prisons effectively under staffing and related political and budget pressures. There are a plethora of organizations and individuals ready and willing to advise the Prison Service on how suicide could be reduced. Various of these are covered in the next chapter looking at some of the key bodies concerned from the Ministerial Council, Harris Review, Prisons and Probation Ombudsman and the Howard League for Penal Reform. But if officials, at times, appear defensive this may, at least in part, reflect the political context of such dialogues. The political dynamic being that one group or other raises issues with Ministers, Ministers in turn ask their officials to respond. The officials then give a response for Ministers and the various relevant groups are then informed of the Ministerial response. This may be a costly and time-consuming process, sometimes for all concerned. There needs to be some careful thought about the distribution of resources across the functions of service delivery and regulation and comment.

Prisons Service Instruction (PSI) 64/2011

There is a PSI document to cover the overall management of prisoner suicide (Ministry of Justice, 2011). For this chapter, we draw primarily, but not exclusively, upon, that in describing the germane policies. The aims are set out straightforwardly at the beginning of the policy document to identify, manage and support prisoners and detainees who are, it says, at risk of harm to self, others and from others. The policy also aims to reduce the incidents of 'self-harm' and deaths in custody. The core of the approach seems to be an understandable focus upon the support of effective multidisciplinary case management to include the sharing of information to reduce incidents of 'self-harm'. Refreshingly, the document contains some mandatory actions, which are helpfully italicised throughout. But what is not clear is the mechanism for ensuring the enactment of the mandatory actions. And this may go some way in explaining the frequently reported mismatch between policy and practice on the ground in prisons. This is perhaps more indicative of a more general management challenge than it is specific to the management of the suicidal. Nonetheless, in this context the cost of this is likely to be at least some preventable deaths of prisoners. Making improvements to the quality of prison management has the potential to impact very positively upon the management of the suicidal. Prison Governors clearly need support if they are to provide the leadership needed to address the issue of prisoner suicide. For example, the need for the observance of the management discipline to ensure the enactment of policies on suicide prevention and be able to demonstrate the checks and if necessary remedial actions that are in place. Staff need to be held accountable for their (in)actions. There needs to be a culture of accountability. Such accountability includes both recognition for successful work and an increased appetite for learning lessons from any such cases. There has perhaps been some frustration that mistakes are sometimes repeated across cases. This can sometimes be reflected, in, for example, the Prisons and Probation Ombudsman's reports.

Assessment, Care in Custody, Teamwork (ACCT)

The administrative process for the management of suicidal prisoners is called, Assessment, Care in Custody, Teamwork (ACCT) documentation and process. The policy asserts that good staff/prisoner relationships are essential to encourage the disclosure of suicidal feelings. This is an important recognition and is why we have touched upon it elsewhere in this book. It is critical that prisoners feel able to disclose their (suicidal) feelings if prison managers are going to ensure that the appropriate support is in place. And the way in which services or roles are structured may influence the level of likelihood of such disclosures or otherwise. These challenges are referred to in more detail elsewhere, especially in relation to the potential role conflicts (see *Chapter 1*) in impacting upon the likelihood of disclosures about suicidal thoughts and feelings to psychologists (Towl and Walker, 2016). Such problems are not insurmountable but they do need to be acknowledged and carefully addressed. But to return to the genuinely challenging issue of what should be a matter of national prescription, in the care of the suicidal, and what should be left to local judgements mindful of the particular nature of the prison, prison staff and prisoner needs? For illustrative purposes, we could look at anti-ligature and cut down procedures. There is currently a national prescription regarding the precise cut down tool which we are informed in the PSI must be a 'Big Fish (9mm)' tool. Yet it appears to be a matter of local discretion as to whether or not staff are issued with such tools. There is, of course, a palpable nervousness around the issuing of such equipment in view of the alternative uses they may be put to especially perhaps in a prison environment, such as weapons.

Prison managers have a level of discretion around the implementation of procedures to manage suicide prevention. In terms of the more general discourse on prisons which currently seems to be heading in the policy direction of greater management autonomy, it is not clear that this will necessarily, in itself, lead to improvements by way of reductions in the rate or number of self inflicted deaths (SIDs). (Executive) Governor/ Directors/Managers (this is language which is intended to be in recognition of both the public and private sector) put more simply 'prison manager' would be a term that could be used across all sectors. It is perhaps for discussion and debate elsewhere as to why the term 'governor' has been held onto rather than 'manager'. Being a governor of a prison is surely no more nor less than being a prison manager.

Each prison is required to have a Safer Custody Team (SCT) with responsibility for policy and practice implementation. Prison managers are required to appoint a Safer Custody Team Leader (SCTL) on the basis of a combination of their competence and formal institutional authority. There is much emphasis on adapting and applying the information in the PSI to meet local circumstances and needs. But in one sense the term Prisons Service Instruction is a misnomer in that much of it constitutes a series of what amount to structured requests for action in the management of the suicidal. For example, it is emphasised that it is desirable but explicitly not mandatory for staff carrying out supervision to have sufficient breaks! Why would that not be deemed mandatory?

Chapter 2 of the 'Instruction' for staff covers the important area of information sharing. This is a potentially crucial area of policy and practice. Readers of the instruction are reminded that data sharing is a perennial issue, and is one that has been raised by the Prisons and Probation Ombudsman. Staff are reminded of their child protection responsibilities in working with imprisoned 15–17-year-olds. Information sharing is a notoriously difficult area in health and social care. The normative expectation would be that consent would be sought from the prisoner to disclose information, but if it is not forthcoming in a potentially life and death situation the member of staff may use their judgement as to what to share. Issues of appropriate confidentiality and consent are by no means only manifest in prisons it is a broader challenge in, e.g. the National Health Service (NHS) too, particularly perhaps across professional groups.

But arguably, the most relevant chapter contained within the PSI is, 'Risk and triggers'. The overview refers to the notion of risk as probabilistic but the more detailed section on risk gives a broader definition to include hazards. Under the section on 'Risk' distinctions are made between dynamic, static, stable and chronic risk factors with an exhortation to consider the use of translation services if the prisoner does not speak English as a first language. Risk factors are listed for violence, suicide and 'self-harm' separately. For our purposes, we will focus upon the section in relation to suicide. Factors are collected together under five sub-headings: demographic factors, background history, clinical history, psychological and psychosocial factors and current 'context'. What is striking about the overall list is the commonality with the list and that of the characteristics of the prisoner population. And this is an important point in illustrating the difficulty of the task of identifying those most vulnerable to suicide at any particular point in time. To take one example from each of the first four categories; low socio-economic group, childhood adversity, mental illness diagnosis and relationship instability. This serves to powerfully illustrate that in terms of such factors they are unlikely to serve any meaningful discriminatory function, the prisoner population characteristics are linked to increased probabilities of the risk of suicide. This would be so too if they were not imprisoned. So, perhaps the key section of the document in relation to 'risk factors for suicide' is the section on the 'current context'.

In terms of the 'current context' the most historically and internationally robust finding from the suicide in prisons literature is reflected in the first bullet point, namely, 'Early days in custody and following each transfer'. The prominence of this variable in the documentation for risk assessment may go some way in us better understanding the under-reported significant success of Prison Service staff in reducing the percentage of those completing suicide early during their imprisonment. This is an area where the research has been applied largely effectively. Such significant achievements could be even better if a similar discipline was observed in the application of other areas of the research base too. What is especially helpful about the inclusion of this bullet point under 'context' is that not only is the focus upon the early days of custody but it is made clear that this is the case following each transfer which is very important to include. The Select Committee on Prisons Safety (2016) was not persuaded by this achievement despite the evidence in support of it. This was regrettable because, amongst other things, the danger is that if successes are not recognised this can lead to staff demoralisation. But also, it may lead to a change in policy, which lacks such evidence to inform it. As is argued in this book, if we are to reduce rates and numbers of suicides in prisons then there needs to be a more nuanced and evidence-informed approach to the well-being of prisoners. In relation to suicide, the prison environment can be especially toxic for imprisoned women. This is perhaps most powerfully illustrated given that their rates of suicide are markedly increased in comparison with women in the community. This effect of proportionately higher rates in prisons than the community is far more marked for women than men. That said, the number of cases that the calculation of the rates is based upon is about 20 fold larger for men.

Probably the most striking omission in terms of the evidence from the current context section is the offence type of sex offending, both violence and arson are helpfully mentioned as flags for an inflated risk of suicide. This is especially striking given that there are more prisoners with sex offence convictions imprisoned than ever before. The percentage of prisoners who are convicted sex offenders has grown since the early-1990s and if we also take account of the more or less doubling of the prison population then we can see how this population characteristic change alone could account for some of the predicted increases in suicide numbers and rates. There may well be intersectional impacts too. That is, some of the characteristics associated with a higher level of suicidality, may interact in important ways. For example, we know that older men have higher rates of suicide in prisons and, in recent years, there has been some growth in older men being imprisoned for sexual offences. The other variable from the research, which could be added to the contextual list are sentences over ten years. Again, there may well be some intersectional impacts but it is worth being mindful of, and warrants inclusion in the list.

There is a section on 'triggers' to guide staff as to what may be possible factors linked with an inflated risk of suicide. Changes in sentence status and transfers between prisons are helpfully highlighted. The importance of transfer between prisons is important to mention because there can be a common misconception that prisoners are only most vulnerable when they begin their sentences. This is inaccurate. An associated myth is that remand prisoners are at an inflated risk of suicide when compared with sentenced prisoners, which is another myth chiefly supported by methodologically limited studies using a snapshot design.

The point about changes in sentence status included in the documentation, is important too, especially perhaps for life-sentenced prisoners who are very much over-represented in the suicide figures. Indeed, the temporal pattern of self-inflicted deaths for life sentenced prisoners is different to that of determinate prisoners in that instead of there being a very significantly inflated rate of suicide in the very early days of imprisonment or transfers there are statistical spikes associated with the point at tariff and thereafter associated with the timings of the decision-making process around whether or not to progress or release or otherwise.

On the section on gender there are some changes needed. It is asserted that 'females' — a term curiously preferred in Criminal Justice over 'women' are less likely to take their own lives in custody. First, as indicated previously the risk of women completing suicide increases at a much greater rate for women when imprisoned than for men. Second, the sample sizes for women in making such estimates are much smaller and so we need to be cautious in making such interpretations. On the most recent research, the rates for men although greater than for women are only marginally greater so it is probably unwise to include it as a meaningful difference in such a list for staff.

A whole chapter is dedicated in the guidance to peer support. It is just over 25 years ago that the Samaritans first trained prisoner Listeners. Although Samaritan-based schemes are not the only schemes they were the first charity to institutionalise such an approach. The advice in the instruction is that the Safety Custody Team Leader (SCTL) provides the management oversight of such arrangements in support of overall prisoner suicide strategies and practices. In view of the widespread implementation of Listener schemes based on the Samaritans approach and the 25 years of system experience there is further guidance for staff provided separately (Samaritans, 2012). Each Samaritans branch where Listener schemes are provided in prisons have, according to the policy, a Branch Prison Coordinator and also a Regional Prison Support Officer. Samaritans who are not prisoners themselves also provide some listening capacity, although this is recognised in the policy, it is also acknowledged that such services are very limited. The Samaritans themselves rightly highlight not only the benefits of Listener services in contributing to suicide prevention but also the benefits to those who are Listeners themselves. Another support scheme, which is perhaps less well-known, is also covered briefly in the instructions — the Insiders scheme. In short, the this is a scheme which involves training prisoners aged under 18 to provide basic information and reassurance to new prisoners who are their peers.

Chapter 5 of the instruction to staff covers the documentation around the management of suicidal prisoners. Once identified, the importance of completing the documentation and undertaking the first case review meeting is emphasised. This is an area of the policy which it appears may not always be enacted in a timely manner. The turnaround times for opening the ACCT is 24 hours and the case review according to the policy needs to happen within 24 hours of that. The guidance for the ACCTs includes a list of tasks to be undertaken by the ACCT team. A 'caremap' is produced for each prisoner with detailed and time bound actions to reduce the risk of suicide. The ACCT plan is kept on the wing that the prisoner resides on and follows him or her if they move wing or prison. The prison manager has the accountability to ensure the quality control of such documentation. Unfortunately, there appears to be some variability with this in practice. The instruction is not perhaps as prescriptive as it could be to be fit for purpose.

Another area with little prescription is that of the make-up of the multidisciplinary team. This seems to be a vulnerability of the policy. There is guidance included on the location of those prisoners who are identified as at an inflated risk of suicide. The use of safer cells is mentioned and this includes the useful caveat of the need to see such safer cells complement rather than replace other approaches to supporting suicidal prisoners. The Prison Service as an organization does not have a national record of how many 'safer' cells there are in the prison system. There is significant variability across prisons as to the availability of 'safer cells'. Helpfully there is the inclusion of advice around closing an ACCT. In practice, there can perhaps sometimes be a reluctance to close an active ACCT. There is particular guidance around the movement of prisoners to other prisons if they have previously been managed and supported under ACCT arrangements, this is a crucial part of the document.

A whole chapter in the PSI is devoted to 'constant supervision'. The instruction indicates that constant supervision should only be considered as a response to an immediate suicidal crisis. The lines of accountability in the management of such cases do not look entirely clear in the instruction with both what is referred to as a 'daily operational manger' and 'senior clinical manager' being able to authorise constant supervision. The lead clinical consultant is referred to as being able to provide advice to the daily operational manger or senior clinical manager. What is unclear is whether or not the responsibility for the staffing of constant supervision can be assured to be implemented, if a senior clinical manager rather than a prison officer manager authorises it. Problems of accountability have sometimes bedeviled the Prison Service where there can be tensions between claims of a 'blame culture' on the one hand and on the other their being 'no apparent accountability', in terms of individual consequences for staff who have been found not to have done their jobs, in some cases of self-inflicted deaths where it appears evident that a life could have potentially been saved.

It is interesting that although the PSI was due for review and reissue in January, 2016 a decision appears to have been made to completely overhaul PSIs across the piece. This is partly in recognition of broader system changes. Currently there appears to be an appetite in government for greater prison manager authority rather than the more traditional centralist organizational structures. Additionally, a new training package on mental health and suicide prevention has been piloted in some prisons. Currently there appear to be some operational challenges in implementing such training. If prison managers are given more autonomy, it will be interesting to see what priority they give to such work to save lives. This perhaps returns the reader to the question of whether or not suicide prevention training should be mandatory or not.

Psychologists working in prisons are very well placed to undertake work on suicide prevention but in recent years much more of their time appears to have been spent with a focus on the risk of harms to others rather than a risk of harm to the prisoner herself or himself. But psychologists do still work with the suicidal in prisons, it is just that in terms of overall workloads it is not given the priority of, for example, sex offender treatment group work programmes aimed at reducing the risk of re-offending. As noted previously, regrettably such programmes have not even been convincingly shown to reduce the risk of sexual offence reconvictions In view of this there is a growing case, perhaps, for the redeployment or re-purposing of such psychological staff to other areas, for example suicide prevention. It is important to remember that the challenge here is not one of low staffing per se but rather their current deployment which does not reflect the importance, and value, of suicide prevention, in comparison with sex offender treatment programmes.

The case of sex offender treatment is used for illustrative purposes but other activities which take up the time of psychologists could also be looked at in terms of their relative importance in comparison with suicide prevention.

Psychologists are able to potentially contribute at a number of key levels. Arguably at the moment, the most pressing is in the area of staff training. This is a very large gap in current practice with a very high need in terms of skilling-up and informing staff. But other areas include policy formulation at national, regional and at the level of the individual prison too. Then there is the area of clinical practice too. So, three areas for the contributions of psychologists are key; policy, staff training and clinical practice.

Psychological contributions could include a focus on evidence-informed approaches again at a national, regional and local level. A national and regional lead psychologist on suicide prevention could be appointed with a remit to provide policy advice, staff training and clinical interventions with individual prisoners too.

This book would be one example of a potentially useful resource for staff to draw upon in policy development and also staff training and clinical practice. Influencing policy formulation is key if there are to be significant improvements with regard to suicide prevention in prisons.

CHAPTER 6

Political and Expert Commentaries on Prisoner Suicide

Introduction

Ministers and service providers are by no means underwhelmed with advice on how to more effectively deliver policy and practice in reducing prisoner suicide, far from it. In trying to capture the range and depth of such perspectives in this chapter included is coverage of the structure and organization of the Ministerial strategic management arrangements along with some of the contributions of some key stakeholders, namely; of the Independent Advisory Panel on Deaths in Custody, Prisons and Probation Ombudsman, Prisons Inspectorate and Howard League for Penal Reform. Each have much to say about how we may reduce self-inflicted deaths in prisons in view of their unique positions and contributions within Criminal Justice. The chapter draws to a close with some of our own recommendations for structural and cultural reforms.

The Ministerial Council on Deaths in Custody

The three tier Ministerial Council on Deaths in Custody was announced in July, 2008 following on from the Fulton report earlier that year (Fulton, 2008). The creation of the Council was a recommendation from the report to replace the previous 'Ministerial Roundtable on Suicide' with a more structured and focused approach to this important work. The three tiers include; the Ministerial Board on deaths in custody, the Independent Advisory Panel (IAP) and a practitioner and stakeholder group. A general strength of the structure is that it is departmentally cross cutting and includes the Department of Health, Home Office and Ministry of

Justice. The core aims are twofold, to reduce the number and rate of deaths in custody. The remit of the council includes all deaths, which, occur in prisons, police custody, immigration detention, the deaths of residents in approved premises and the deaths of those detained under the Mental Health Act. Prisoner suicide will remain firmly the focus for this chapter.

The broader remit of the group is one of the distinguishing features from the structural arrangements that preceded the setting-up of the council. The membership includes Ministers (who chair) and officials from each of the three departments, which, in practice, can sometimes be a strength, and sometimes a weakness too. A strength, because when departments are working effectively together the whole may be more than the sum of the parts in view of the departmental interdependencies. A weakness in the sense that three sets of officials and ministers need to be involved in decision making and sometimes this results in marked delays and inaction where there is agreement and, of course, sometimes there is not sufficient agreement. Those included as part of the Board are; the Association of Chief Police Officers (ACPO), the Care Quality Commission (CQC), HM Inspectorate of Prisons, HM Inspectorate of Constabulary, Howard League for Penal Reform, Independent Custody Visiting Association (ICVA), Independent Police Complaints Commission (IPCC), Inquest, NHS England, Office of the Chief Coroner, Office of the Children's Commissioner, Prisons and Probation Ombudsman (PPO), Prison Reform Trust (PRT), Samaritans, Independent Monitoring Boards (IMBs), Coroners' Society of England and Wales, Youth Justice Board (YJB) and UK Immigration and Detention (UKID). It is evident, from such a snapshot that there are a broad range of stakeholders with an interest and involvement in deaths in custody in general and self-inflicted deaths in prisons in particular. The range of organisations involved also perhaps gives a hint of the costs invested into such activities. A point that will be returned to later in the chapter is whether or not there is any learning about the balance of funding between these various bodies and service delivery in suicide prevention. Again, in terms of making a difference to policy and practice developments the relatively broad range of contributors to this body may be both a potential help and, at times, hindrance. It can be helpful because of the range of expertise and experience and a hindrance in that there may be a broad range of views and understanding of the evidence, on how best to inform policy and practice to reduce deaths in custody. But essentially, this tier of the board brings together the key Ministerial decision makers with the listed stakeholders having an opportunity to have potentially significant influence.

The second tier of the council is the Independent Advisory Panel (IAP) which has a chair and five members. Toby Harris was the first chair of the IAP followed by Kate Lampard on a temporary basis whilst Juliet Lyons was appointed to the post, officially in September, 2016. Projects undertaken either by the IAP or on its behalf are included on its website at iapdeathsincustody.independent.gov.uk

The third tier is the practitioner and stakeholder group, which is much wider in its reach than the other two tiers to ensure broader stakeholder engagement and expertise.

There is a secretariat that provides the administrative support for the three tiers. In 2014, Ministers commissioned a review of self-inflicted deaths in prisons for those aged between 18 and 24. The review was chaired by Lord Toby Harris and is generally referred to as the Harris Review. Members of the IAP were also members of the Harris Review team.

The Ministerial Board has provided the overall leadership in this challenging area and the Independent Advisory Panel has produced annual statistical reports on deaths in custody in addition to various reports covering a range of factors associated with deaths in custody more broadly. There has been engagement with the third tier but this has perhaps been less evident since around 2014.

It was always intended that the IAP would provide the engine room of expertise to the council. A number of the projects undertaken since the formation of the IAP reflect the particular expertise of its members. And there is much commendable and important project work, which has been successfully undertaken. But what there is not is a sense of strategic direction nor a sense of place and function in relation to the range of bodies, inhabiting this policy and practice influence upon Ministers. The terms of reference for the IAP provide an elaboration of the purpose of the overall council. In particular, the IAP is required to act as the primary source of independent advice to Ministers and service leaders. Curiously for an advisory body, part of the remit involves the monitoring of compliance with any guidance and standards issues. This is curious because it is surely more properly the role of line management within the relevant organization, here HM Prison Service.

The appointment of a new chair was announced in August, 2016 in an upbeat statement which was linked to an assertion that Ministers were providing the National Offender Management Service (NOMS) (from 1 April 2017 HM Prison and Probation Service) with around £10 million of funding to reduce deaths in prison custody. This affords the Prison Service a potential opportunity to make a step change in the quality of care for the suicidal in prisons. In her role as temporary chair of the panel Kate Lampard was asked by Ministers to undertake a review of the panel in keeping with a broader practice of triennial reviews, which is the Cabinet Office process for reviewing the functions and activities of Non-Departmental Public Bodies (NDPBs). A review was sent to the Secretary of State for Justice in April, 2016. One possible outcome appears to be a greater alignment between the work of the IAP and the board (IAP, 2016). Hopefully there will also be a move towards having more of an international focus to the work to better understand the wider context of the problem of prisoner suicide and also contribute to, and learn from, broader international discussions and debates focused upon the evidence and learning in relation to prisoner suicide.

So, that is the overview of the existing structures and organizational arrangements in terms of the Ministerial strategic leadership. Of course, the Prison Service is responsible for implementation and this aspect is addressed separately in this book in *Chapter 5* on 'The Management of Suicide in Prisons'. Next, there is an overview of some of the findings of the Harris Review, one of the most comprehensive evidence-informed reviews of prisoner suicide in the history of prisons.

The Harris Review

'And no one should be under any illusions, prisons and young offender institutions are grim environments: bleak and demoralizing to the spirit'—Lord Toby Harris, Chair of the Harris Review, Foreword to the Harris Review, p.4.

The above quote would not be out of place in a Charles Dickens novel. This is not to suggest that improvements in the physical conditions of prisons have not been made. But it is widely recognised that there are still too many Victorian prisons. Prisons can still be squalid environments, which are a burden to the human soul. The human condition of imprisonment psychologically remains much the same. There are many more prisoners and staff (than in Victorian times) but the essential dynamics of incarceration remain the same. Prisons are impervious institutions.

One striking feature of prisoners and their visitors is their financial poverty which stands in marked contrast to prison staff albeit prison officer pay has been devalued over recent years, prison governors, doctors and psychologists remain relatively well paid at levels which put them with incomes which are typically well above the UK median income. We have seen that by contrast prisoners disproportionately experience high levels of unemployment before, during and after their imprisonment. Indeed, the experience of imprisonment, all things being equal, most probably increases their chances of being unemployed upon and after their release. As we have seen elsewhere (see *Chapter 4*) prisoners tend to have relatively poor life chances.

The above is the rather grim backdrop to the findings of the Harris Review, which was probably the most detailed review of 18–24-year-olds, in prisons and young offender institutions that has ever been undertaken, internationally. The reason for the focus on this age group was a recognition that chronological age does not necessarily equate to maturational age and emotionally young prisoners may be developmentally delayed in comparison with more financially advantaged groups. We know that the rate of suicide in prisons amongst this age group is typically lower than for other prisoners however, the numbers of completed suicide are relatively high in view of the overall age profile of the prisoner population.

The review team began work in April, 2014 with the submission of the final report going to Ministers in July, 2015. One key, albeit unsurprising conclusion of the review was that there are not enough activities for young prisoners to participate in in prisons. We know that unemployment is linked to higher rates of suicide so it is no surprise that in replicating this situation within a prison we may well be increasing the risk of suicide further. One distinctive feature of the report is the recommendation for a new statement of purpose of prisons. There is a clear frustration in the report between what is euphemistically referred to as, 'A disconnect between what those in charge think should be happening and what is actually happening', p.10 Harris Review. And this may well be a general problem for many orgnaizations with nationwide services and distributed systems. However, with sucide prevention, some mismatches may sometimes contribute in matters which are literally life or death.

A key systemic recommendation of the review was to divert more young people from imprisonment. Interestingly there seems to be a growing political consensus that we need to reduce the prison population if we are to most effectively address reducing reoffending. One central plank of the review was a recognition of the high levels of needs of prisoners, with a particular focus upon the 18–24-year-old groups.

Structurally the Harris Review strongly recommended that the powers of the Prisons and Probation Ombudsman should be strengthened and under the auspices of Parliament, rather than the Ministry of Justice. Again, there was a palpable frustration that despite recommendations made, in many cases prison staff were not completing the ACCT documentation in a number of examples of completed suicide. Arguably of all such deaths these are some of the more predictable and preventable, thus this is all the more a matter of concern that this sometimes continues not to be enacted. Prison managers make decisions which may impact upon the relative prioritisation of such work.

Government Response to the Harris Review

The government response to the Harris Review appeared five months later in December, 2015. It read like a party political statement on the state of prisons rather than as a specific response to the Harris Review. The response does successfully cover some of the laudable initiatives to improve the prison system, but too much of it simply seems to be about the issuing of instructions rather than a demonstration of some of the weaknesses of the system as identified in the Harris Review, e.g. the evident 'disconnect' between central instructions and enactment. Some of it reads rather vaguely, 'The Youth Justice Review will be informed by the Harris Review', p.14. There comes a point when the reviews need to stop with a focus instead on delivery rather than further reviews. But the government response does give broad agreement on the importance of a focus on prevention, but in a rather circumspect fashion. There is a sense in which the response rather overplays the importance of tackling new psychoactive substances in addressing prisoner suicide. The focus seems to be on consequences for prisoners in more of a punitive than therapeutic tone. It would have been perhaps a more positive approach to commit to the provision of useful activities for prisoners to engage with. This is perhaps especially so given the evidence on the potential consequences in relation to mental health outcomes with unemployment.

Despite unemployment being linked to an increase in the risk of suicide the government response asserts that data will not be collected on time spent engaging in purposeful activities. This comes across as a disappointing rejection of an entirely reasonable proposal. The, arguably, implausible claim is made by government that collecting such data would serve no useful purpose. It is difficult to see why there would be no interest centrally in having data on the levels of prisoner activities in prisons. But there seems to be more than no interest, there seems to be a wish not to have the data perhaps reflected in the following aspect of the response, 'this would be unduly time consuming (it would currently require costly manual data collection)'. It would be great if a response would reflect the leadership need to embrace the opportunities afforded by, for example, data digitalisation. Unemployment remains a major mental health hazard with a link to an increased risk of suicide. Employing prisoners in meaningful work whilst in prison would be one way of further reducing the risk of completed suicides in prisons.

So, overall a delayed and mixed response from government. In sum, broad agreement around the need for earlier interventions but disagreement around the importance of data to inform leadership decision-making in the Prison Service.

Prisons and Probation Ombudsman (PPO)

The PPO undertakes independent investigations into complaints and also deaths in custody. As previously we will focus solely upon the brief for investigations into self-inflicted deaths in prisons although recognising that the remit of the PPO is wider. The purposes of such investigations include understanding what happened, to correct injustices and identify any lessons to learn. For the most recently reported year (2015/2016) of activity in investigating self-inflicted deaths in prisons these totalled 103. This was significantly up on the previous year (2014/2015 — 77) which has served, in recent months, to intensify the political and media focus upon self-inflicted deaths in prisons. Although the PPO is operationally independent of the Ministry of Justice (MoJ) it is sponsored by the MoJ. This is an anomaly, it would surely make far more sense for the PPO to be independent of the MoJ in every sense. One of the significant administrative achievements of the PPO in recent years has been to achieve the delivery of all reports into self-inflicted deaths in prisons on time. Another achievement is the production of a series of documents, which focus upon 'lessons learned'. One key report, for illustrative purposes, from the perspective of the student of suicide in prisons is a report produced in 2015 (Prisons and Probation Ombudsman, 2015). What may be learnt from it?

The report has as its focus a comparisons of the data from one year to the next, 2012/13 to 2013/14 with the year of data running from April to the following March for each year. A number of 'lessons' are helpfully listed in the report. The importance of seeking evidence of factors associated with an inflated risk of suicide is highlighted. And there is an important distinction to be made here. Which is that interview data from the prisoner is one source of evidence, which needs to be viewed alongside other data sources too. The second lesson highlighted is that of, at risk of stating the obvious, a need to ensure that all prisoners receive an induction or introduction into the prison. Regretably and to the evident frustration of the author this does not always happen. Later we will look in more detail about the normative expectations of another body, the prisons inspectorate, with regard to such matters, which gives a more detailed sense of what may be needed for inclusion in 'induction'. The third lesson emphasised is that of the need for an improved continuity of care, and an awareness and responsiveness to changing prisoner needs. The fourth lesson listed is that of the first month being a period of particularly heightened level of risk of death by suicide. Restrictions on family contact are also identified as another factor associated with an inflated risk of suicide. The Incentives and Earned Privileges (IEP) regime which is imposed upon prisoners is also mentioned as a potential contributory factor which is interesting partly because it was in 2013 that a more austere (or severe) version of the IEP was introduced. And this raises a number of fundamental (ethical) questions about what as a nation our philosophy is of imprisonment. The IEP regime brings into sharp focus debates around what may be deemed 'privileges' or normative expectations, for example, with the use of in-cell televisions. Decisions around such matters also perhaps reflect the value put on those imprisoned in our society.

The issue of the potential inappropriate segregation of prisoners is tentatively touched upon as one of the lessons learned too. The learning exhortation being that prisoners on an open ACCT document are only put in segregation under truly exceptional circumstances. Linked to this, the challenge that many staff appear to find in working with prisoners who may be both aggressive whilst also being vulnerable is alluded to. The final 'lesson learnt' refers to the importance of individualising the plan for the prisoner. This has parallels with some offender risk assessments, which can be made in relation to life sentenced prisoners where global categories are used to 'target', e.g. problems with alcohol insofar as it may generally be linked to an increase in a propensity to violence amongst some cohorts. It is important to take an individualised approach to such assessments. But one of the often unspoken problems is that

staff, have simply not had the level of education or professional training required to do this aspect of the job anticipated of them. Suicide
prevention training is not deemed a priority in comparison with other
demands against a general backdrop of a growing prisoner population
and diminishing staff population.

In term of the research data presented comparing the recorded characteristics of the prisoners who had completed suicide there were no
surprises in terms of what we know from the extensive suicide in prisons research literature. The data on sentence length would have perhaps
benefitted from more clarity in terms of the allocation of prisoners to the
sentence length boxes because of the overlapping categories used. Prisoners with a two-year sentence could have been allocated to one of two
parts of the graphical representation of the data. But this does not amount
to a material problem, more a matter of detail, which may have had a
potentially significant impact with a larger sample or population size.

But perhaps the key and most disappointing, but illuminating, finding from the research was that despite being identified at an inflated
risk of suicide, a number of those prisoners who were being managed
under the ACCT system exposed a gap between policy and enactment.
In other words, only 40 per cent of those identified had had the required
case reviews, which surely reflects poorly on prison managers — this
is a process where there seems to be insufficient evidence of effective
local management. And, as we shall see, this reflects a key finding of
the Harris Review — the significant gaps between policy and practice.
As the PPO rightly points out highlighting that the ACCT system is
not being implemented is nothing new, albeit it is very concerning. An
earlier review of ACCTS from 2007 to 2012 had found that about half
of all ACCTs had not been implemented correctly. Presumably, in view
of this evidence and the current challenging operating environment all
senior management teams in prisons will have ACCT management as a
standing item on their (meeting) agendas.

HM Inspector of Prisons

Unlike the PPO, HM Chief Inspector of Prisons (HMCIP) has statutory
responsibilities, which are fundamentally about reporting to the Secretary

of State on the treatment and conditions of imprisonment. Again, as with the PPO remit the range of work of the inspectorate is wider than that of this book, hence we still focus upon self-inflicted deaths in prisons and not, for example, in immigration removal centre or secure training centre which both come under the remit of the inspectorate.

HMCIP make explicit much of their methods for inspecting prisons through the issuing of inspection criteria. These include a section on safety, which is perhaps of particular political and operational relevance for 2017 in view of 2016 having been a challenging year in terms of ensuring the safety of prisons for prisoners and staff. The safety section has a subsection on 'self-harm' and suicide prevention. But there is another section, which is also directly pertinent—a section on respect, which we will also touch upon in this section. Interestingly, and perhaps a product of its time and establishment tradition, the default position seems to be for the expectations sections to be referring to men with a separate and parallel set of documentation with regard to expectations in terms of women prisoners.

Expectation 12 is that the prison under inspection is a safe and secure environment. The indicators of the delivery of this expectation are largely helpful particularly with regard to the exhortation to recognise the specific needs of particular groups with an emphasis on the early days of custody. This chimes with the need to further nuance policy and practice to reflect the research especially in terms of prisoner risk profiles and needs. The indicators included by the inspectorate essentially reflect Prison Service policy and in practice inspectors will, in significant part, be checking whether or not policies have been enacted appropriately. There are some helpful areas of cross-reference made with the indicators, e.g. substance misuse, bullying and violence reduction and resettlement. There is considerable overlap with what the PPO investigators look at in relation to their reports on completed suicide. This is to be expected. It is not clear why there is a separate ombudsman and inspector both charged with aspects of suicide prevention activities.

Included in the 'respect' section is a clear focus on the importance of good staff prisoner relationships. The importance of everyday courtesy is listed as the first indicator for treating prisoners with humanity and respect. In one sense, it reflects poorly on the Prison Service that an inspector needs to cover much of the interpersonal territory of needing, for example, to refer to prisoners using their preferred name or title and never to use insulting nicknames or derogatory or impersonal terms. Historically some prison officers seem to have found this basic requirement extremely challenging which may speak loudly of a punitive culture, which can sometimes underpin the interactions of prison officers with prisoners. Research in the 1970s in prisons identified the differing ideological cultures of different staff groups (e.g. Parsloe, 1976). It is a poor reflection on the culture of prison officers that an inspector of prisons feels the need to include indicators of humanity and respect such as, 'cell cards and the unit roll board list the first and second names of individual prisoners' in the 21st-century. Surely it would be axiomatic that that would be done? Similarly, it is of grave concern that the Prison Officers' Association, in a 2017 dispute, defined suicide prevention work as a 'voluntary task' (*Guardian*, 28th February 2017. 'Justice secretary wins injunction to stop prison officers' industrial action'). Clearly this is not an issue about resources, but rather perhaps one about prison officer culture, a culture which can sometimes still seem out of step with rehabititative expectations. Prison mangers need to tackle this directly as part of their commitment to suicide prevention.

It is to the credit of the chief inspector of the day that a further and separate list of expectations have been drawn up through consultation to reflect some of the distinctive needs of women in prisons. Refreshingly, the introduction to the expectations asserts the limitations to the document, namely that, 'even if every expectation in this volume is met, large institutions, often far from home, are a far from perfect way of meeting the needs of the very vulnerable women who make up so much of the female prisoner population in England and Wales' (Chief Inspector of Prisons, 2014).

The version of the indicators under suicide and 'self-harm' include reference to those who are pregnant, post-natal or separated from their children too. Victimisation is mentioned but not revicitmisation, which could be important for a number of women prisoners in terms of their experiences in prisons. There are also expectations for the staff gender

114

mix in working with women prisoners with HMCIP checking for at least 60 per cent women staff.

Howard League for Penal Reform (HL)

A key thrust of the campaigning of the HL has been to reduce the prisoner population. This is one clear way in which the number but not necessarily the rate of suicides would be likely to decrease. Reducing the prisoner population would also potentially free up staff to undertake fuller roles in working with prisoners. It would also ease, potentially and considerably, staffing pressures.

The HL and Centre for Mental Health have produced a report entitled 'Preventing Prison Suicide' (2016). In their work, they draw from the reports of the coroners in England who published 'Prevention of Future Deaths' reports, the Harris Review and an HMCIP annual report published in July, 2015 raising concerns about the number of self-inflicted deaths. They also refer to the Prisons and Probation Ombudsman (PPO) learning lessons reports and finally the work of the Justice Select Committee on prison safety. The HL draws from the structure used in Prisons Inspectorates reports, both organizations sharing a focus upon a concept of a 'healthy prison' an approach derived from earlier work by the World Health Organization (Howard League, 2016).

In their report, they assert that all prisons need enough skilled staff. But they seem to use the term 'staff' as synonymous with 'prison officers'. This appears so too with the research quoted in support of the need for more (skilled) staff. The researchers not only discovered that staff/prisoner relationships were key, but also, it seems, broadly, when they asked prison officers if they needed more prison officers they said yes. Some would say, they would do, wouldn't they.

The HL helpfully highlight the issue of the tensions between the Incentives and Earned Privileges scheme and the needs of prisoners in terms of their risk of suicide particularly during the early period of imprisonment. And there is a palpable tension between the two sets of policy. For example, the restriction of visits and telephone contact with family seems deeply unhelpful in terms of suicide prevention and more likely to contribute to the promotion of prisoner suicide. This point is made compellingly by the HL.

Also raised is the problem of there being, at times, too many prisoners held in segregation units who have been identified as suicidal. The Prisons and Probation Ombudsman also raises this issue and HMCIP too, yet it still seems unduly common according to the HL, who gave evidence to the Supreme Court on this matter. The HL commend the work of the Samaritans through prisoner peer Listener schemes in prisons but note that some prisons do not have sufficient numbers of Listeners in view of the scale of need. The HL have called for reduced prisoner numbers. This may very well result in an increase in the rate of suicides. This is because a number of those groups over-represented in the completed suicide figures are broadly for more serious offences, which would be highly unlikely to attract a community sentence instead of a custodial one. Hence if overall numbers were cut back the proportion of those imprisoned for more serious offences would constitute a proportionately larger group of the overall prisoner population. However, crucially, in terms of the absolute numbers of suicides, all things being equal, a concomitant decrease in the numbers of suicides would most probably occur. Abolishing the current Incentives and Earned Privileges scheme for more positive alternatives that are less restrictive especially for the early days of imprisonment are also persuasively advocated. Further investment in ensuring that the role of the prison officer is a rewarding and fulfilling occupation is also argued for by the HL. Finally, the need for cultural change is advocated for, so that prisons can be healthier environments for prisoners and staff alike.

Reflections upon the ideas to reduce suicide of the IAP, PPO, HMCIP and Howard League

There seems to be a general agreement across these four groups at least that one way of, amongst other things, reducing the numbers of prisoner suicides is to reduce the prisoner population. There also seems to be a general concern about the rules around Incentives and Earned Privileges (IEP) and the tension between these and the best interests of prisoners in reducing their risk of suicide particularly for the early period of imprisonment. The sometimes explicit and sometimes implicit exhortation made seems to be the need for a change in culture and all such parties seem to argue for an increase in staffing levels (which could be achieved in relative terms simply by cutting prisoner numbers). The reference to such increases seems to be focused exclusively or perhaps chiefly upon prison officers.

If suicide prevention is to be more successful then there is a need to reduce prisoner populations and government and the courts have a primary role with this. Also, there does need to be a consideration of abolishing the IEP system, at least in its current form. On staffing there is scope and need to employ rehabilitative staff, currently there is, it seems, an undue focus upon prison officer staff increases. Allied health professionals need to be considered as staff groups to contribute to improving outcomes with prisoners, they are rarely mentioned yet constitute a significant proportion of, for example, the NHS workforce.

Readers may wish to consider the findings of the PPO on the completion (or otherwise) of ACCTS and also the oddity of the wording of HMCIP with regard to some specific indicators giving expression to the expectations that the inspectorate reasonably has for the treatment of prisoners and conditions of prisons. For example, under the expectations report section on 'respect' subsection 9. It reads, 'Staff address prisoners using their preferred name or title and never use insulting nicknames or derogatory or impersonal terms'. It is extraordinary that it should be normative to check for such conduct, this suggests to us some fundamental concerns about prison culture. This aspect of the culture is problematic for suicide prevention. HMCIP may wish to make that link more explicit in their documentation.

More staff are needed in prisons. But we would argue that a more productive approach in terms of addressing negative aspects of prison culture would be to introduce more allied health professionals broadly construed to focus upon prisoner support and welfare. In public health terms this would be a great opportunity to get services to those most in need. If government is serious about safety and rehabilitation, then a shift in the culture seems key and a fundamental change of the staffing profiles is what may help. Prison officers could also be given further and fuller training to help enact what may be termed the 'welfare and wellbeing' aspects of their roles too. There would need to be appropriate volumes of staff to make this work. Whereas when it was announced that 2,500 more prison officers were to be recruited this was generally welcomed this, in and of itself, is not likely to be a sufficient change to make a tangible difference to the rates of suicide in prisons. There is perhaps a need for staff who are skilled in working with prisoners in addressing personal and welfare needs. The opportunity would be to introduce staff who are not primarily focused upon security issues in the rather restricted way that is sometimes the case with managers and prison officers as if care and control are mutually exclusive variables. The primary focus of such a new cadre of staff would be on welfare and rehabilitation.

In terms of immediate actions addressing the issue of those on indeterminate public protection (IPP) through immediate release where appropriate to do so would be one step. Redeploying staff employed as psychologists to work primarily in prisoner induction areas to address the welfare needs of prisoners could well help. This would not be an issue of additional resource but rather a re-deployment of existing staff. This would probably mean moving a large number of psychologists from high security prisons to local prisons. This could be done without new resources and with no added risk to the public.

Also, do we need to dispense with the title 'prison governor' and replace it with a more generic 'prison manager'? There is a parallel with work we undertook in psychological services in prisons between 2000 and 2005. Previously the term 'prison psychologist' had been used to describe the role of applied psychologists working in prisons. This was changed to reflect the need for parity of esteem and quality of services with professional psychologists elsewhere in the private and public sector. The most common type of applied psychologist was a forensic psychologist in prisons and thus the 20th-Century term of 'prison psychologist' had virtually disappeared, sending out a clear message that the complexity of the role is not about place but function. Effective prison managers are just that. This is important because the prison service may benefit from getting more managers in to manage prisons with experience from a range of sectors. Just as the term 'prison psychologist' seemed an anachronism to us the term 'governor' does too, best dispensed with. Such changes may seem minor but they send powerful messages of strategic intent. In psychological services this led to the first ever, strategic framework for applied psychological services and very significant improvements in psychological staff retention ('Driving Delivery, A Strategic Framework for Applied Psychological Services', 2003).

There also needs to be more emphasis on learning from the existing research. The field is currently awash with research. The challenge is both strategic in term of how services are best structured, and operational, in terms of addressing policies and cultural factors which are at odds with effective suicide prevention. Senior management need to ensure and assure themselves, and others, that appropriate policies are not only crafted but implemented and monitored and managed accordingly.

CHAPTER 7

Suicide in Prisons: Early Literature

Introduction

This chapter provides an overview of some of the early empirical studies into suicide in prisons. The focus is primarily on research in the United Kingdom but key international research is also covered.

Reviews of suicide in England were undertaken from the foundation of modern public sector prison systems in the 19th-Century. These were largely descriptive and the first empirical study of suicides in England and Wales is generally taken to be that by Topp (1979). This built on early studies looking at issues of prison welfare, often undertaken by prison reformers. It is perhaps striking that empirical studies into prison suicide took so long to develop and that concerns around suicide, and indeed prison conditions more generally, typically came from outside of prison systems.

In addition to Topp (1979) two early studies undertaken in Australia can be seen to have had a marked impact on later research. Undertaken in the 1980s this research was in part a response to growing public and political concerns about high death rates in Australian prisons.

Early empirical studies

The research undertaken by Topp (1979) is often cited as the first modern study into suicides in prisons in the UK. However, Topp (1979) begins with a review of early studies into suicide in prisons in England and Wales, most notably the work of Smalley (1911).

Taking a more empirical approach Topp (1979) calculated trends in the rates of suicide in prisons, based on officially recorded suicide statistics.

These were calculated for the period 1880–1971, based on seven-year intervals. The total number of deaths recorded as suicide for this period was 775. The rate of suicide was reported to range from 28 to 60 per 100,000 prisoners per year. This was calculated based on the 'Average Daily Population' (ADP) in prison per year.

Topp went on to conduct a more detailed analysis of the available written records on a smaller sample of 186 male prisoners, assed to be self-inflicted deaths between 1958 and 1971. The average rate of self-inflicted deaths for this sub-group was reported to be 13.3 deaths per year. The overall rate was reported to be 42 per 100,000 ADP and 14 per 100,000 receptions, between 1958–1971.

Of the 186 cases reviewed 69 (37 per cent) were on remand and 63 per cent were sentenced. Most the sentenced prisoners (56 per cent) were serving sentences of 18 months or longer. Topp also reported that a majority (77 out of 186) of killed themselves within the first month of custody; going on to note a progressive decline in the rate over time reaching a baseline level at around the fourth month in custody. Of the sample studied 90 per cent were found to have had previous criminal convictions and 64 per cent had previously been in custody.

The study found no clear patterns for the time or month of death, save only that Saturday seemed to be a more common day for deaths to occur. In turn it was noted that around 38 per cent of the sample had a history of contact with mental health services, with around 30 per cent having been admitted to mental hospital. This suggested much higher levels of severe mental health problems than seen in the general prison population. Of those with histories of mental health contact, around ten per cent had a history of 'depressive episodes'. In addition, 51 per cent of those with a history of contact with mental health services had a history of suicidal behaviours, with around 20 per cent having multiple incidents. In around a third of cases the interval between the latest incident of suicidal behaviour and the act which caused death was found to be less than six months.

In his study Topp (1979) went on to make several observations on the continuity of what might now be termed 'social exclusion' and death in prison custody. This included the finding that in 82 per cent there were indications of unstable relationships, in 79 per cent the person was single or separated, 54 per cent had been living in short term rented accommodation, or were homeless prior to their arrest. In the sample studied 45 per cent had no known contact with relatives or friends, 38 per cent had a recorded history of parental deprivation before the age of 16, 30 per cent had a drink problem and 11 per cent had a drug problem. It is perhaps worth noting that in this period drug use in the UK was much lower than presently, so the level of 11 per cent represents a much higher level than was generally seen.

Building on the early findings of Goring (1913) and the results of his study, Topp (1979) suggested that the idea that the early period of custody was a time of risk were confirmed by his study. The first month in custody appeared to be a time of markedly elevated risk. He also suggested that those serving longer sentences were more likely to complete suicide. In contrast to some early work Topp (1979) made the argument that a high proportion of those completing suicide in prison were suffering from some form of 'psychiatric disorder'. He went on to suggest that a high proportion of self-inflicted deaths were, in large part, linked to poor impulse control and attention-seeking behaviours which went wrong. He suggested that 59 per cent of those who died in his study could have had some expectation of being saved and at least half seemed to have acted on an impulse. He went on to speculate that several those who died may have been making attempts to elicit sympathetic attention, and when these failed they escalated their attempts to a dangerous level. Putting aside what some may see as his apparent contempt for these suicidal prisoners, the study is an example early work built upon by others.

This study and the ideas suggested went on to be widely cited and informed later policy development, in a manner that earlier work had not perhaps done. Specifically, it led to a greater stress on the role of health care staff and specifically medical practitioners in seeking to identify those at risk of suicide.

The study did though suffer from several methodological weaknesses. Most notably perhaps, the failure to operationally define many of the methods and terms used, in a manner that would allow for replication. Indeed, in parts this makes interpretation of the study impossible. Most critically the study involved an analysis of suicides and 'probable' suicides. The basis for deciding why these were determined to be 'probable' is not though made explicit, introducing the potential for unintended biases in the sampling.

With hindsight though it appears this research had three main influences on the area of prison suicides, it stimulated further research, influenced the direction of that research and informed policy and practice in prisons in the UK until the early 1990s.

Further work was undertaken in the 1990s (Dooley (1990a; 1990b) based on analysis of written records, covering all cases of unnatural death occurring in prisons in England and Wales from 1972 to 1987. An analysis of written case records for prisoners receiving a verdict of suicide in a coroner's court was undertaken, involving 295 cases. The analysis was based on general Prison Department files. This analysis has been criticised for relying on poor quality information. Later research noted that these general Prison Service files depended heavily on self-report from the prisoner, with very limited information being available from other sources, particularly in the early stages of custody (Jones, 1996; HM Chief Inspector of Prisons, 1999; McHugh, 2000).

These studies divided the period under study into four-year intervals. The rates of suicide were calculated for these intervals in terms of Average Daily Population and by Receptions. This suggested a very marked increase in the level of suicide, with an 81 per cent increase in suicides per 100,000 ADP and 80 per cent by receptions into prison.

Based on the limited information available, the findings in relation to social exclusion appeared to echo the earlier findings. Around 26 per cent appeared to be of no fixed abode, or were living alone at the time of reception into prison. Equally the majority had previously been in prison and 74 per cent had previous criminal convictions recorded. Almost a third had a history of mental health contact and over a quarter had previously been in a mental hospital. Alcohol abuse was common with 29 per cent having a recorded history of alcohol problems and 23 per cent illicit drug use. Around a quarter of the sample had received some form of psychotropic medication in the month before they died. In 97 cases where a previous mental health history was established 22 per cent had an identified psychotic disorder, 23 per cent had been treated for depression, 26 per cent were identified as having a personality disorder and 26 per cent as having drug addiction.

In terms of sentence length, a significantly greater proportion were serving longer sentences, of more than four years. Over 25 per cent had been sentenced to life imprisonment.

Interestingly a high prevalence of intentional self-injury prior to death was noted, with 43 per cent having some record of self-injury on their prison service file and 22 per cent having a record of such injury during their current custody.

Unlike Topp (1979) no differences were reported for deaths by day of the week. Almost 50 per cent of the deaths though were recorded to happen between midnight and 8 a.m., with the remainder spread evenly throughout the day. Findings reported by Topp (1979) and Hatty and Walker (1986) in relation to time in custody were replicated. In this study, around 17 per cent of the suicides occurred within one week of reception into prison and 29 per cent within a month, suggesting that the early period after reception into prison was a time of heightened risk.

Several conclusions were draws from this work. Firstly, it was suggested that the period on remand (i.e. where someone was imprisoned but not convicted) was a time of increased risk. Secondly, the role of 'mental illnesses was stressed. Thirdly, the mixed motivations involved for those prisoners who killed themselves in prison was stressed.

The research completed by Dooley (1990a; 1990b) can be seen to have had a significant effect on policy and practice. The research has though been subject to several criticisms. Most strikingly it has been noted that the quality of the data involved was poor. The available written records in general prison service files were often incomplete and even where they were not, they were often heavily reliant on uncorroborated self-report. The reliability of such data is generally very variable, and is often poor for those recently received into prison (McHugh, 2000).

In addition, and crucially, the research included only cases receiving a coroner's court verdict of suicide. There are several problems with such an approach as it introduces systematic legal biases, that have little to do with the behaviour of concern. This in turn generates problems of interpretation that, based on the reported information, are insoluble. The under-representation of women in the reported suicide figures may, for example, be the result of coroners being more reluctant to return suicide verdicts on women than men (Towl and Fleming, 1997).

Equally the reported high rates of suicide in prisoners with a history of mental health contacts may be a result of coroner's courts being more willing to record these deaths as suicide. The presence of some clear mental disorder, may make it easier to overcome the legal test of beyond reasonable doubt for a suicide verdict.

Australian studies

A questionnaire-based study looking at 155 deaths in Australian prisons between 1980–1985 as reported (Hatty and Walker, 1986). Of the deaths studied 77 had received official verdicts of suicide. The other deaths had received verdicts including misadventure, accidental death and death by natural causes. The researchers went on to compare these two groups. They reported a higher death rate for women than men (3.3 per 1000 per year compared to 2.5) and higher levels of suicide verdicts (1.7 per 1000 per year compared to 1.2). They go on to note that any conclusions in this area need to be tentative, given the small number of women in custody. The results for the means of death were like those reported in earlier prison studies, with hanging being the most frequently seen form of death. This was followed by heart disease, which accounted for around 16 per cent of male deaths but no female deaths.

In looking at the effects of age the Australian researchers concluded that the rates of death appeared to increase with age and were especially high in the over 50 years of age groups. Given that the study included natural deaths from coronary heart disease, this finding is perhaps not surprising. In contrast though prisoners receiving suicide verdicts were more likely to be younger and were particularly in the 20–24 age range. The over-50s age group though also appeared to be over-represented relative to their numbers in the prison population.

Ethnic background also appeared to be a significant factor in Australian prisons, with those of 'aboriginal' descent showing a 50 per cent higher rate of deaths. In addition, this group showed more deaths in the under 35 years' groups. The rates for suicide deaths though was reported to be similar for aboriginal and non-aboriginal prisoners. This contrasts in one sense with UK studies that have largely found ethnic minority groups to have lower rates of self-inflicted deaths than white prisoners.

Overall Hatty and Walker suggested that in Australian prisons the difference between deaths recorded as 'suicides' and other deaths was modest. In both groups, they reported that homicide offenders were greatly over-represented.

Several criticisms have been made of this research. In common with others the researchers reported results as if they have compared all deaths (including suicides), with the suicide group. If this was the case then it represents a significant error, in that some prisoners would be considered in both comparison groups. In deriving the descriptive statistics, this would serve to mask any differences. The researchers give limited detail on statistical analyses, so it is unclear whether this was in fact the case and if so whether the researchers were aware of it and made efforts to correct for this.

It has also been suggested that, given the sample size, the research was overly ambitious in dividing the data into too many sub-groups, for example, analysing multiple offence types. This resulted in several very small samples, limiting the extent of meaningful empirical analysis.

Hatty and Walker suggested that their findings supported the previously reported findings that those on remand were over-represented in suicide figures, relative to convicted prisoners. They also noted that they were similarly over-represented in the overall mortality figures.

This conclusion has though been questioned by several later researchers. It has been suggested that such excess mortality in remand prisoners, may, more plausibly and frequently, be a facet of the way rates have been calculated (Dexter and Towl, 1995; Bogue and Power, 1995; Towl and Crighton, 1998). Turnover of remand prisoners is known to be much higher than for sentenced prisoners. Remand prisoners may be received into prison for relatively short times before being bailed or found not guilty at trial. But there remains in some of the literature, reflected in the professional practice of some psychiatrists, psychologists and nurses that remand is, in and of itself, a marker of inflated risk of suicide. The danger of this belief is that an equally 'at risk' individual with the legal label of 'convicted' may appear to have a lower risk when this is not the case empirically. An additional complexity is that some individuals may experience multiple periods of remand in prison custody. The overall result though, is that a larger number individuals will be placed 'at risk' in prison by being detained on remand, compared to sentenced prisoners over the same time. Historically this was not adequately addressed in calculations of rates of deaths in custody. In looking at the Scottish Prison Service, Bogue and Power (1995) corrected for the higher through flow of remand prisoners and found that the excess rates of death seen for remand prisoners disappeared. This finding was replicated in studies of suicide in prisons in England and Wales in the 1990s (Crighton and Towl, 1998; Crighton, 2001). This suggests that the early concerns about remand as a risk factor for suicide may well have been chiefly a product of method of calculation rather than reflecting true differences. This is a finding and conclusions which differ fundamentally with the most recent study in this area by the office of the prisons and probation ombudsman (Prisons and Probation Ombudsman, 2014).

What does seem to be true is that some groups of remand prisoners show high levels of suicide. Those remanded on homicide and sexual charges show high rates of self-inflicted deaths. This parallels the higher rates found in those who went on to be convicted of homicide and sexual offences (Towl and Crighton, 1998).

Notably 85 per cent of suicide deaths in the Australian study occurred during the first ten per cent of the prison sentence. In contrast, deaths from other causes tended to be spread evenly through the sentence.

A later study in Australia (CSC, 1988) presented an analysis of deaths in the state of Victoria in Australia over a five-year period. The study derived from concerns over the markedly higher rates of suicide in this group of prisons, when compared to the rest of Australia.

The researchers began by noting a marked increase in the rate of suicides in New South Wales prisons between 1982/3 and 1983/4, going on to reduce to previous levels in 1984/5. The overall level of suicides in prisons in Australia was reported to be around seven times higher than for the general population. In part this reflected the fact that prisoners are not drawn randomly from the community and present with a higher incidence of characteristics known to correlate with suicide. These would include the fact that prisoners tend to be disproportionately male, unmarried, of low occupational status or unemployed, have weak family or community ties and tend to use more alcohol and drugs.

The study looked at deaths in prisons between 1 January 1980 and 31 December 1984. A total of 35 deaths were analysed, 19 of these having received a verdict of suicide. A total of 20 of these deaths had occurred in two establishments. It was found that 90 per cent of the suicides and 38 per cent of the other deaths occurred in the prisoner's own cell or dormitory. Most deaths happened at night, with suicides tending to be between 5.30 to 8 p.m. or 1 a.m to 5 a.m. Those who killed themselves also tended to be in single cells (95 per cent). This contrasted with the fact that almost half the relevant prison population at that time were housed in dormitory conditions. Efforts to place all prisoners in single cells have been motivated by a desire to improve conditions and sanitation in prisons. In relation to suicide though, placing prisoners alone in small cells, dominated by integral sanitation may have been counterproductive. In future, more creatively designed accommodation may be useful in reducing suicide and other risks. As with other research the first month of custody appeared to be a time of heightened risk, with 26 per cent of deaths recorded as suicide occurring within a week of reception. Those convicted of offences against the person and especially homicide was over-represented amongst suicides.

Based on a review of available medical files for a sample of 15 of the 19 deaths recorded as suicides, five were known to have received psychiatric treatment or consultation during the current term of imprisonment. This compared to three of those dying of natural causes. Two were diagnosed as schizophrenic, one as having schizophrenic symptoms, and one as drug induced psychosis.

Prison suicide: studies of self-injury

The most influential studies of this type derive from the work of Liebling (1991). Her work was comprised of two parts and drew on current theoretical work in sociology and criminology. The research involved both semi-structured interviews with prisoners and the use of participant observation methods, to analyse factors contributing to risk of self-injurious behaviours. A series of interviews with 100 young offenders, located in four young offender institutions in England and Wales, were undertaken. Of these 50 had a recent history of intentional self-injury and 50 were chosen at random from the prison population. Self-injuring prisoners were drawn from those who had been referred to the healthcare centre for treatment and there were 34 men and 16 women in each of the groups.

The research suggested several significant differences between the subject and control groups. The group who had self-injured tended to be serving longer sentences than the controls. They had also received less positive reports at the pre-sentencing stage in court. These two findings suggest that the subject group may have been, in some important respects, a distinct population.

The family backgrounds of the subject and control groups also appeared to differ in several respects, with the control group surprisingly reporting more unstable family backgrounds than the subject group. In contrast the self-reported histories of mental health assessment and treatment and of familial histories of suicide and attempted suicide, were higher for those who had self-injured. Interestingly this group reported higher levels of being in local authority care. They were also more likely to have received mental health treatment, as either in or outpatients.

An association between substance abuse and suicide and intentional self-injury has often been suggested (e.g. Backett, 1987; Topp, 1979) and here the subject group had more serious difficulties with alcohol use and were more likely to have experimented with a wider range of substances both legal and illicit. They were also more likely to have a drug abuse related index offence.

The subject group reported higher levels of intentional self-injury outside prison. This group were also more likely to report such behaviours as being 'suicide attempts'. A small number of those who had repeatedly self-injured did not characterise their behaviour as suicidal.

Both the groups had trouble in adjusting to imprisonment, with feelings of anxiety being common. High levels of boredom were also noted, especially in those who self-injured. This may reflect the fact that they were less likely to be involved in constructive activities in custody, some-thing that was exacerbated by the closure of education services over the Summer, during the period of the study. This meant that individuals faced long periods in cells.

Other differences between the groups also emerged. A higher pro-portion of the subject group reported a dislike of physical education (30 per cent vs. four per cent). The subject group also appeared to have fewer internal resources and reported finding it more difficult to find constructive things to do when in their cells, with around a third saying they could find nothing at all to do compared to only four per cent for the control group.

In seeking to explain this difference, Liebling (1991) developed the notion of 'coping' as a central hypothesis of her early research. She sug-gested a crucial interaction in the context of intentional self-injury, between the environment and an individual's own resources. To an extent this mirrors the work of Williams and Scott (1988) in relation to depres-sion, where the interactions between the person and the environment are fundamental.

This study produced several interesting observations. A higher pro-portion of the subject group reported finding prison based staff to be unhelpful (22 per cent versus 14 per cent). Strikingly both groups tended to find staff helpful, suggesting that positive staff contact may have been protective. The subject group are also reported to have had more com-plaints about the Prison Service disciplinary system, and were more likely to have been given solitary confinement as a punishment. This finding has been reflected in the comments of the Prisons and Proba-tion Ombudsman, with the observation that prison officers struggle to interpret need and potential threat alongside each other (Prisons and Probation Ombudsman, 2014). The difference between the two groups may have been how the prisoners were treated by prison officers.

Prison visits also appeared to be important and both groups reported anxiety around these. A minority in both groups reported receiving the full allowance of visits and both groups reported problems with visits. Overall though those who self-injured reported having fewer visits and writing fewer letters. They also reported missing specific people more than the control group.

The model developed by Liebling to account for such self-destructive behaviours was based on the notion of 'coping capacity'. This has though been subject to concerns about its conceptual circularity. If a prisoner is suicidal, it is deemed that they are 'poor copers' yet if they are 'poor copers' then they are more likely, so the theory goes, to complete suicide. Most significantly it has been suggested that the model places undue stress on within individual characteristics, at the expense of environmental and situational factors, which arguably can be particularly powerful in a prison environment. Psychological research in this area has suggested a dynamic interaction between the individual and the situation they find themselves in. There is also a well-observed tendency for observers to under-estimate the contribution of situational factors in behaviour, particularly where the outcomes of the behaviour are negative (Eiser, 1980).

Not surprisingly perhaps interviews with Prison Service staff tended to identify the role of pre-existing vulnerability prior to reception (sometimes called the importation hypothesis by researchers). Bullying was often cited by prisoners, as a contributory factor in intentional self-injury by prisoners but staff were reluctant to accept this explanation, without qualifications. Intentional self-injury was though widely thought by prison officers to often be a means by which young offenders could escape from difficult and potentially threatening situations. Almost two thirds of the staff interviewed for the study did not feel that young offenders made the most constructive use of their time in custody.

This research had a marked impact on policy development in prisons in the UK. Most strikingly suicide and self-injury came to primarily be an issue for the prison, rather than, as previously, a health care matter. As such the primary response and responsibility for suicide and self-injury was placed largely on prison officers.

Studies of completed suicides

A study based on a sample of deaths that occurred in Scottish Prison Service establishments was conducted by Bogue and Power (1995). This study included deaths that were legally defined as suicide between 1976 and 1993; a total of 83 deaths. Of these written prison records were available for 79 cases.

An analysis of the trends over time suggested that there was a marked increase of around 40 per cent in the rate of suicides, in Scottish Prison Service establishments.

For the period 1980–93 the researchers found that those aged over 30 years were significantly over-represented in their sample.

The study looked in detail at the effects of legal status and the notion that those on remand were at elevated risk of suicide. In doing this the study replicated previous findings that remand prisoners were significantly over-represented as a proportion of Average Daily Population (ADP) in prison. However, the researchers were critical of the previous interpretations of this finding noting that, when the rates of suicide for remand prisoners were calculated based on reception figures, the apparent over-representation in the suicide figures was no longer evident. They went on to suggest that reception figures provide a much better estimate of the number of remand prisoners placed at risk in the prison environment. In this key respect, they noted that the suggestion that remand served as a risk indicator for suicide was flawed and the level of risk was similar or lower than for sentenced prisoners, when the number of individuals placed at risk was accounted for.

In Scotland longer sentences seemed to be linked to higher rates of suicide, with a significantly level of those be serving sentences of more than 18 months when compared with the general adult sentenced prison population based. Linked to this perhaps a higher proportion of those completing suicide had committed or been charged with violent or sexual crimes, in comparison to the Scottish prison population.

In common with previous research both in the UK and internationally, a high proportion of suicides took place during the early stages of custody. Two thirds of deaths recorded as suicides took place in the first three months in custody and over four fifths within one year. Strikingly around a tenth killed themselves within less than 24 hours of reception into custody.

A series of key studies in prisons in England and Wales were conducted in the 1990s (Crighton and Towl, 1997; Towl and Crighton, 1998;

Crighton, 2000). These studies began by addressing key definitional problems that had been a limitation of much of the earlier research into suicides in prisons. Primarily this involved applying similar terms and definitions to those used in the broader public health field (see Charlton et al 1992a; 1992b) and using operational definitions for suicide based on World Health Organization criteria for self-inflicted deaths. In turn this allowed for more meaningful comparisons with community and international rates, albeit still with some caveats.

The relevance of this was clearly illustrated. For the period 1988–1995 the proportion of self-inflicted deaths by men in prisons in England and Wales, recorded as suicide verdicts, ranged from 58 per cent to 84 per cent (McHugh and Towl, 1997). For women from 1988–1996 the overall rate was markedly lower at 27 per cent (Towl and Fleming, 1997).

Many researchers have identified background factors thought to be associated with an increased risk of suicide. These include factors such as disrupted family backgrounds, familial histories of suicide, drug and alcohol abuse, poor school performance, unemployment and depression (Diekstra and Hawton, 1987; VanEgmond and Diekstra, 1989). It is striking how closely such factors reflect several the 'social factors' identified in prospective studies of criminal careers (e.g. Farrington, 1993). Such factors also tend to be associated with prisoner populations (Towl and Crighton, 1996). In this sense the prison population includes a disproportionately large number of individuals who may be at a higher risk of suicide than average. Unemployment has been found in community studies to be associated with increased rates of suicide Platt and Kreitman, 1984; Moser et al 1984, 1990). Interestingly, two key studies indicated that the unemployment rates immediately prior to imprisonment were very high (Dexter and Towl, 1995, Jones, 1996) report rates of 77 per cent and 76 per cent respectively.

Two important limitations to several of these studies on suicide are striking. First, many are based upon small sample sizes (e.g. Dexter and Towl, 1995). Secondly, several studies have focused on a specific population sub-group, such as young offenders (e.g. Liebling, 1991) or those located in a single establishment (Jones, 1996). Both factors of necessity limited the generalisability of the results obtained. Towl and Crighton's study went some way to countering such critiques by using a large sample (n=377) and providing an analysis of all self-inflicted deaths, across all parts of the Prison system (i.e. adults, young offenders and women prisoners).

Towl and Crighton outlined several findings from their research. Firstly, they suggested that there was a general trend towards greater sentence length being associated with completed suicides. In contrast to Hatty and Walker's study they found that Life sentenced prisoners in their study were over-represented in relation to the number of Life sentence prisoners.

In common with Bogue and Power, Towl and Crighton noted the powerful effects of the method of measurement used in calculating suicide rates amongst remand prisoners. When they calculated rates for remand prisoners using the average daily populations (ADP) the rate appeared high (238 per 100,000 ADP per year). In marked contrast, when the rates were calculated using the number of deaths by remand reception numbers into the prison the rates are very markedly lower (39 per 100,000 receptions per year). They compared this to the rates for determinate sentence prisoners. These ranged from 31 to 75 per 100,000 ADP per year. This led them to conclude that remand prisoners are at a similar risk of suicide to those given short determinate sentences (under 18 months) and are at a lower level of risk than those given longer or indeterminate sentences.

The Prison Environment

The different functions of different categories of prisons are reflected in their 'regimes'. In local and remand prisons, there is a high 'throughput rate' amongst prisoners to and from the courts, as well as other prisons. Such 'throughput rates' tend to be lower in other prisons. This, it could be argued, is likely to be an important factor in understanding suicide in prisons (Crighton and Towl, 1997; Towl and Crighton, 1998).

Most deaths (65 per cent) in the latter study occurred in local or remand prisons, with much lower rates being seen in category C training prisons (10 per cent), youth custody centres (nine per cent) and dispersal and Category B training prisons (both eight per cent). They did not though calculate the rates of completed suicide for different types of establishment, based on receptions. It seems likely that this may, to some extent, explain the proportion of deaths in local prisons.

The authors reported that in 71 per cent of cases death occurred whilst the individual was in a single cell, compared to 23 per cent located in shared cells. In seven per cent of cases this information was not recorded. They reported that there were no recorded cases where death occurred whilst an individual was in a ward or dormitory setting in prison.

They went on to test the hypothesis that younger age groups (i.e. 15–24 years) would be over-represented in the figures for prison suicides. They argued that there did appear to be some evidence, albeit limited, to support this hypothesis (for children) in the juvenile group those between 15 and 17. In general though younger age groups did not appear over-represented. This finding was also evident in earlier findings, based on smaller samples, examining suicide data in prisons for the periods 1988–90 and 1994–95 (Crighton and Towl, 1997).

Previous work by Dexter and Towl (1995) had highlighted the importance of the social context in seeking to understand suicide in prisons. Various aspects of prisons, they suggested, may effectively serve to increase or decrease the risk of suicide for individual prisoners. In support of this is the observation that prisons with similar roles may show very different outcomes, based largely on the specific institutional culture. Aspects of the organisation of prison regimes appeared to be having marked impacts on suicide rates. Around two thirds of suicides occurred in local prisons and these tend to be the busiest and often most impersonal institutions. There was at that time a lack of any adequate research into the effects of high turnover of population on prisons culture. High throughput within an establishment it was suggested was likely to disrupt social contacts and increase uncertainty amongst both staff and prisoners. These effects may be amplified when the overall prison estate gets full as is the case currently (2017) when prisoners are simply allocated to any available places rather than be able to take account of issues such as the travelling distance of families for visits or other related considerations.

The early stages of custody have been associated with high rates of suicide, and the first two months or so within a prison appeared to be of significance. This view is supported by research in Scotland (Bogue and Power, 1995) and England and Wales (Crighton and Towl, 1997).

Other studies have identified factors that may impact on suicide rates within regimes (Dexter and Towl, 1995; Jones, 1996). Both studies suggested that positive and constructive staff attitudes towards prisoners seemed to be particularly significant. The importance of staff attitudes in suicide prevention has been highlighted and reflected in studies of staff training programmes (Lang et al, 1989; Cutler, Bailey and Dexter, 1997).

In May 1999 HM Inspectorate of Prisons published a thematic review of suicide and self-injury in prisons in England and Wales (HM Inspectorate of Prisons, 1999). This influential report was to set the tone for much of the following decade. This built on an earlier thematic review by Stephen Tumim the then HM Chief Inspector of Prisons (HM Chief Inspector of Prisons, 1990) and focused on the period 1988–98. Over this time there had been a marked increase in the number and the rate of self-inflicted deaths in prisons for England and Wales. The rate of deaths per 100,000 of ADP went up from 54 in 1982 to 128 in 1998.

The largest single rise in the rate for self-inflicted deaths was seen for those on remand and this was greater than would have been expected from the increase in numbers. In terms of the rate per 100,000 receptions the most marked increase was seen from 1996 to 1998 was reported as being seen in the convicted and unsentenced population. Here an average increase of 250 per cent was reported, although this was based on a small number of cases.

The report's authors also went on to analyse self-inflicted deaths by establishment type and offence type. They reached the conclusion that the rate of completed suicide amongst women prisoners was broadly in line with their representation in the prison population (i.e. they represented 3.5 per cent of suicide deaths and four per cent of the prison population).

In contrast, they suggested that those charged with sexual or violent offences were over-represented relative to their proportions in the prison population.

Previous findings in the United States had suggested that black prisoners were at relatively lower risk of suicide than white and Hispanic prisoners (Haycock, 1989). This was replicated for the first time in the

UK with black prisoners showing lower suicide rates than white or Asian prisoners (see Crighton and Towl, 1997; Towl and Crighton, 1998). This finding has been subject to suggestions in the USA that white and Hispanic prisoners find prison more stressful, a view which has been firmly rejected by Haycock (1989). In the UK Towl and Crighton (1998) suggested that the effect may be a result of discrimination in the criminal justice system, with black prisoners showing fewer risk factors for suicide.

Secondly, they noted that younger age groups did not appear to be over-represented. The age distribution of self-inflicted deaths was found to be broadly like that of the prison population. This was also seen in a sample of attempted suicides and incidents of self-injury. Looking at the year 1996–97 the distribution appeared to be in line with the population with one exception. Those in the 21–29 years' age group appeared to be slightly over-represented.

Using a sample of data provided by the Prison Service's Suicide Awareness Support Unit (SASU) the authors also analysed the time from reception into prison to the time of death. The results of their analysis again replicated the findings of several previous studies, which suggested the initial period after reception was one of greatly increased risk of suicide. Indeed, the first 24 hours was identified as a time of exceptional risk.

In fact, this it could be argued that this somewhat oversimplified the pattern seen in prisons. The available evidence suggested that the initial 24 hours after reception were indeed a time of exceptionally high risk. The level of risk though appeared to remain high well beyond the initial 24 hours, only levelling out after around three months from reception into a new establishment (see Towl and Hudson, 1997; Towl and Forbes, 2000).

The authors also looked at the role of psychiatric disorder in suicide. They concluded that the area has been bedevilled using poor and shifting definitions. In turn this had served to make valid conclusions difficult. They suggest that high levels of 'psychiatric morbidity' seen in prisons may in fact make this a less useful indicator of possible risk than in the community.

Conclusions *Chapter 7*

Recent studies into suicide in prisons have been characterised by increasing methodological sophistication and a greater willingness to draw from community-based studies. The results of this have included an increasing use of operational definitions, which in turn has made comparisons between studies more meaningful. The greater influence of community studies has also served to put suicides in prisons into a wider context. It can be convincingly argued that such changes have led to much more relevant and applicable research, which has challenged some prior notions about suicide in prisons.

In common with several research studies in the community there has been a trend in studies of suicide in prisons to view suicide as the extreme end of a continuum of self-destructive behaviours. If accepted this enables researchers to directly question those who have engaged in such behaviours and extrapolate their findings to suicide. This approach has characterised several studies into suicides in prison. However, it does need to be pointed out that the evidence for (or against) the fundamental assumption underlying this approach remains highly questionable. At present, it remains a hypothesis.

It is important that studies of those who have gone on to complete suicide have also developed. Such studies have, of necessity, drawn upon written records of suicides in prison. They have, to date, also suffered from several methodological weaknesses. These have included problems in producing and applying operational definitions of suicide as well as a tendency to report studies based on small sample sizes.

Even so several consistent findings have been reported from such studies. Firstly, the initial period in custody has been shown to be associated with high rates of suicide. Researchers have variously identified the initial 24 hours, the first week and the first three months in custody as being periods of risk.

Initial notions of remand legal status being associated with high rates of suicide have increasingly been called into question. More recent research suggests that early findings in this area reflected the method by which rates were calculated, more than they reflected real differences.

The role of 'mental illness' in suicide has also been increasingly questioned. This area has suffered from an ongoing failure to define terms, along with ongoing changes in mental health law and practice. What does seem apparent is that whilst those experiencing 'mental illnesses are as a group at greatly increased risk of suicide, in the context of prisons (and the community) they represent only a small minority of suicidal deaths though.

Whereas the role of 'mental illness' may have been overstated, it does seem evident that many of those who complete suicide in prisons have a history of psychological and social difficulties. These include such things as substance abuse and mild to moderately severe mood disorders, poverty and unemployment.

Two things are striking about the early literature on suicide in prisons. Firstly, it was an area that has received little academic or clinical interest over time. Early pioneering studies in the 19th-Century were not built on and, for lengthy periods, the area was completely neglected. As with community studies it seems likely that early research was held back, to an extent, by the fact that suicide continued to be a criminal offence in several jurisdictions. In England and Wales for example suicide remained a criminal offence until 1961.

A second striking feature of the early empirical research in this area is the slow rate of progress. Early studies of prison suicide in the 19th-Century were primarily and understandably descriptive studies, with only limited efforts at analysis. Some of the studies which followed though, did not show significant development and were methodologically unsophisticated. Linked to this, early studies appeared to suffer from being isolated from wider methodological and theoretical developments in the social sciences and medical sciences generally and in suicide research specifically. It is striking how long this isolation lasted. By the 1980s many methodologically sophisticated studies had taken place in the community and there had been sustained work in theory building. Work in prisons remained curiously isolated from such developments.

CHAPTER 8

Suicide in Prisons: Modern literature

Introduction

This chapter addresses the modern literature on suicide in prisons from around the 1990s onwards to the present. This period saw a marked growth in the research literature and marked developments in methodology and theory. Research into suicides in prisons has increasingly drawn on methodological and theoretical development from other settings. Work since the 1990s can be broadly said to have involved two main approaches. One of these takes as its starting point the assumption that suicide is at the extreme end of a continuum of self-destructive behaviours. This view has a long history and owes much to psychodynamic theorists such as Menninger (1938) and to sociological approaches traceable back to Durkheim (1952).

This has led to the development of studies involving those who have engaged in, or are at relatively high risk of self-injurious behaviours. Such studies can be seen to have many potential advantages. Most notably they allow for investigation techniques such as the use of self-report, that are not available in cases of completed suicide. In turn this has allowed the exploration of areas such as motive and intent. A key question with such studies is though, how far they are applicable and inform our understanding of suicide. If the assumption that intentionally self-injury forms a continuum with suicide is incorrect, or only partially correct, then the relevance of such research to suicide may be partial or the results may be potentially misleading.

The second primary approach has continued to be retrospective studies of those who have ended their own lives in prison. Such studies derive largely from public health approaches to morbidity and mortality (Charlton et al, 1998). They do not rely on looking at analogous behaviours at all but focus on cases of suicide and self-inflicted death. Such studies do have several potential weaknesses. They are generally based on available records and information, all of which may be incomplete or unreliable to some extent. The quality of records on prisoners is often poor and frequently unreliable. It may be collected in haste, it is generally very dependent on uncorroborated self-report from people who may be in significant distress. Importantly such information is also not generally collected with a view to understanding suicide.

A series of largescale studies of prisons in England and Wales were undertaken covering the period 1988–98 (Crighton and Towl, 1997; Towl and Crighton, 1998; Crighton, 2000). The research involved detailed analysis of a total of 525 cases of self-inflicted deaths, which included all those who died in Prison Service establishments, as well as some of those in the custody of private contractors. This constituted a sample of 88 per cent of all deaths between 1st of January 1988 and 31st December 1998.

Gender

Based on this sample of suicides in prison, the research suggested higher rates of suicide in men, as a proportion of the average daily population (ADP) over the decade. Rates calculated on an annual basis showed more variation. Here rates for women were prone to marked variations, largely because of small sample and population sizes for women.

Ethnicity

Reliable data on ethnic origin was only available for deaths from 1994 onwards, based on prisoner's own assessments. Analysis of this provided some support for previous findings which suggested an under representation of black prisoners. The observed rate amongst black prisoners was lower than that for white prisoners or Asian prisoners.

Legal status

Within these studies the rates calculated based on ADP showed that prisoners on remand had much higher rates of self-inflicted deaths. Over the 1988–98 period the rate for remand prisoners calculated using ADP was over four times that of sentenced prisoners. When rates were calculated based on receptions into prison though rates were similar for both groups. This suggests that the effect is a result of the larger numbers passing through prisons on remand rather than this being a risk factor per se.

Mental Health

Around six per cent of those who died were on prescribed drugs for psychotic disorders, suggesting the presence of severe mental health problem. However, this was consistent with the population levels of such mental health problems reported in previous research (Meltzer, Jenkins, Singleton et al, 1999). In this review of mental health in prisoners around ten per cent of men on remand and seven per cent of sentenced prisoners had a history of psychosis. For women, this was higher at 14 per cent.

A history of psychotic disorders did not therefore appear to be good indicator of increased risk of suicide. This contrasts with findings in the community and may reflect the higher rates of mental health problems seen in prisons. Those receiving medication for psychotic disorders were a small minority of the total number of suicides (Crighton, 2000). The prevalence of prescribed anti-depressant drugs was low at 7 per cent. This may suggest that only a small minority of prisoners had been identified as having depression requiring treatment. Alternatively, it may reflect failings in primary health care in prisons with low rates of detection and treatment.

Very high levels of abuse of non-prescribed drugs were found for those who ended their own lives (43 per cent). Most cases involved multiple drugs with some involving combined heavy alcohol and drug use. This suggested a higher prevalence of the use of non-prescribed drugs that seen in the prison population. The study by Meltzer et al(1999) for example had found around 30 per cent of the prison population had a history of substance abuse prior to custody.

Expressions of suicidal or self-injurious intent in prison have often been discounted as indicators of risk. This practice has been extensively criticised (see Dexter and Towl, 1994). Such expressions were often attributed to secondary goals such 'attention seeking'. In relation to prisons this appears to be misplaced and a majority (51 per cent) of those who died had a recorded history of stating their intent to end their lives. In turn this is likely to be an underestimate due to under-recording.

The studies also replicated previous finding that suggested high levels of previous self-injury. Of those completing suicide 45 per cent had a history of intentional self-injury. Self-injury was relatively common in the prison populations then. The study by Meltzer et al(1999) reported lifetime prevalence of 27 per cent and 25 per cent for male remand and sentenced prisoners. For women, the rates were 44 per cent and 37 per cent. The prevalence of self-injury for those completing suicide therefore appeared to be markedly higher leading to the suggestion that self-injury had been under estimated as a risk factor for suicide in prison.

Offence type

Suicide rates were highest for those convicted of violent offences. For this group the rate of deaths was 103 per 100,000 of ADP. Perhaps surprisingly those convicted of drug related offences had a relatively low rate of suicide, at 35 per 100,000 ADP. Those convicted of fraud and forgery also evidenced a relatively low rate of suicide at 39 per 100,000 ADP. Other types of index offence appeared to be similar in terms of the rates of suicide. Those convicted of sexual offences, burglary, robbery and thefts showed rates of 56, 50, 500 and 50 per 100,000 ADP respectively. However, albeit based on small numbers, arsonists appeared to be at greatly increased risk of suicide.

Previous research had suggested that life sentences were associated with exceptionally high risk of suicide. It is not possible to know how many individuals on remand for murder and attempted murder would have gone on to be given life sentences. However, even based on an estimate of 50 per cent, the rate of suicide for this group of untried and convicted unsentenced prisoners was over 700 per 100,000 receptions per year. This perhaps reflects the fact that this group of prisoners are generally seen as the most at risk in custody.

Time in custody

Previous research had consistently suggested that the early stages of custody were a time of increased risk. This was replicated in this series of studies. Annualised rates of suicide were calculated and the results of this were especially stark. The annualised rate of deaths for those who died in the first day after reception was very high, and the rates for days two to seven were only slightly less shocking. From day eight after reception onwards a steady decrease in rates was reported so that by around day 30 after reception the rate of suicides had reduced to what appeared to be a baseline level.

Previous analyses of time in custody can be criticised for being unduly simplistic. The data from this series of studies looked at time since reception into custody and time since reception or transfer into the establishment where they died separately. This showed a preponderance of deaths in the period following shortly after reception. This was largely independent of time in custody.

Care and support

Data reported by the now defunct Suicide Awareness Support Unit (SASU) suggested that around 35 per cent of prisoners had been identified as high risk and were subject to management procedures at some point (McHugh, 2000). Around 65 per cent of prisoners who went on to complete suicide had not been formally identified as being at risk. Around 18 per cent of prisoners were subject to suicide management procedures at the time of their death.

A range of responses to expressions of intent were seen. Most commonly a referral to primary healthcare was seen (42 per cent). Almost all of these requested an assessment by a medical practitioner. Interestingly this is not what staff at that time were required or trained to do in such circumstances. The correct response of opening formal monitoring and support (then called F2052SH procedures) was slightly less commonly seen (35 per cent).

In a significant minority of cases expressions of intent had been incorrectly assessed as not genuine. In turn this had typically been followed by decisions to make no response. This was also seen in several cases where a POL1 (exceptional risk form) had been received. Here exceptional risk had been identified by other agencies in 29 per cent of cases and passed on. This in turn may be an underestimate, as it does not take account of lost POL1 forms.

Around a quarter of prisoners who went on to complete suicide were subject to some form of special observation at the time of their death. No form of watch proved infallible. Around ten per cent of deaths occurring whilst under what was described as 'constant watch'. Most deaths involved those under 15-minute fixed watches, with some being subject to longer intervals. The use of such fixed interval observation has been subject to extensive criticisms, being seen as costly in staff time but largely useless in preventing suicides. It is therefore surprising that this approach has persisted so long in prisons.

Key findings

In summarising the key findings from the series of studies in the 1990s the researchers drew out several themes. They noted that there had been a trend of rapid growth in the rate of suicides. Linked to this they noted that the suicide rates in prison were much higher than those in the community. The extent of this difference is striking when the rates are compared in similar terms. Groups such as male violent offenders showed rates of over 1,000 deaths per million of ADP: compared to typical rates of around 100 in the community.

The rates of death were consistently higher for men. This was true when calculated based on ADP and was more marked when calculated based on the number of receptions into prison. The difference in rates between men and women was though less marked than it is in community studies, possibly suggesting women prisoners have more marked difficulties in areas associated with suicide (e.g. mental health problems).

The research suggested that children in prison (aged 15–17 years) showed higher rates of suicide than young adults (18–24 years). The highest rate though was seen in the 25–49 age group; with the greatest absolute numbers of suicides being in the 25–39 age group. This it was suggested may reflect selection factors operating for younger adults in prison (i.e. they were less selected for factors associated with inflated risk of suicide). The finding may also reflect the age-related trends seen in the community.

In common with North American research black prisoners showed markedly lower rates of suicide than white or south Asian prisoners. It was suggested that may be a result of biases in the criminal justice system with black prisoners who showed lower levels of mental health and other problems being given custodial sentences.

Broadly defined mental health problems were common in those who killed themselves in prison. Serious mental health problems though did not appear a good indicator of risk. Around seven per cent of prisoners who killed themselves were prescribed anti-psychotic drugs, seven per cent anti-depressant drugs, 12 per cent anti-anxiety drugs and five per cent the opiate methadone singly or with other drugs (primarily a 'detoxification' treatment for substance abuse). This suggested levels like the population prevalence in prisons.

A striking finding of these studies was that over half had expressed their intention to kill themselves. Many also had a history of intentional self-injury and around one in ten had an incident of self-injury noted during their current period in custody. Despite this such expressions had often been dismissed as irrelevant.

Those who had offended violently against others were found to show higher rates and those convicted for homicide offences appeared to be at exceptional risk. In contrast, sexual offenders did not appear to be at elevated risk compared to other groups of prisoners. Those charged or convicted for an index offence of fraud and forgery showed markedly lower rates of suicide. Life sentence prisoners and those charged with offences likely to attract a life sentence showed the highest rates of all.

This series of studies found that time spent in a setting was a risk factor for deaths. The first day after reception into an establishment appeared to be a period of exceptional risk, whilst the first week appeared to continue to be one of very high risk. The rate of suicides reduced sharply as a function of time since reception, reaching a baseline level after around 31 days. This appeared to be largely independent of total time in custody, with the change of environment appearing to be the critical factor.

Post-millennial studies

Work into suicide in prisons since the millennium has focused on some of the emerging trends and changes in the prisoner population. This period saw a gradual reduction in overall rates of death from around 2000 until around 2008. This has been followed by a period of marked increase in the numbers and rates of self-inflicted deaths and also rates of serious self-injury.

In 2004 the results of a survey study of deaths over a two-year period was reported (Shaw, Baker, Hunt, Moloney and Appleby, 2004). This involved a total of 172 self-inflicted deaths. In terms of total numbers of deaths, the researchers found that around half were on remand and half sentenced. The initial period in custody continued to be seen as a time of exceptional risk with around a third of the deaths happening within the first seven days. The authors suggested that very high rates of mental disorder were present in those who died at 72 per cent. This finding was complicated by the breadth of definition used, which included drug use as the most common mental health issue (27 per cent). The authors also reported that more than half of those who died showed evidence of mental disorder on reception into prison.

Following on from this more detailed analysis of the role of mental health problems has been undertaken (e.g. Rivlin, Hawton, Mazano and Fazel, 2010). This study looked at a sample of incidents of near fatal suicide attempts in prisons. The authors looked at a sample of 60 cases using a matched group of prisoners for comparison purposes. The authors reported that mental disorder was present in all of those who had attempted suicide and in around two thirds of the control group of non-self-injuring prisoners. They went on to calculate the odds ratios for various forms of mental disorder and found these to be particularly high for depression and psychosis, although the rates were also elevated for anxiety disorders and drug misuse.

A review further review of trends in prison suicide was reported in 2011 (Humber, Piper, Appleby and Shaw, 2011). In this review the rate of self-inflicted deaths in prisoners continued to be, unsurprisingly much higher than in the general population. The researchers looked at the period from 1999 to 2007 and drew on data from the Safer Custody group within the UK Ministry of Justice. A questionnaire study of prison staff was also undertaken.

The researchers found a fall in the overall number of self-inflicted deaths. The rate of deaths in the 18–20-year-olds also decreased. The rates of death in those with issues of drug dependence also reduced. By contrast the researchers found a trend of increasing rates amongst violent offenders.

This work was followed by a case control study in 2012 (Humber, Webb, Piper et al (2012)). This study involved an analysis of all suicides in prison between 2005 and 2008. This involved 220 cases and a sample of 220 living prisoners matched for demographic characteristics. In line with previous findings a history of violent offending was a strong indicator of increased risk. Similarly, they suggested that mental health problems were indicative of increased risk. In line with the findings from the 1990s they found that a history of previous self-injury was much more common in those who killed themselves. In contrast to the work in the 1990s though the authors reported that non-white ethnicity was a predictor of self-inflicted deaths.

Conclusions *Chapter 8*

Research undertaken since the turn of the century has tended to confirm several consistent findings from earlier work, as well as identifying some emerging changes. These have included consistent findings that prisoners are at greatly increased risk of suicide compared to the general population; and that they do not closely resemble the general population. The increasingly large prison population is drawn from the most socially excluded groups. They arrive in prison with a variety of disadvantages and mental health problems. As such direct comparisons with the rates of suicide outside prisons is misleading.

Most of the post-millennial research has involved an essentially public health approach. In this respect, it suggests a move away from more sociological approaches seen in the 1980s and early-1990s. These stressed the need for whole community approaches to suicide and self-injury and reduced the stress on health care assessments and interventions.

It seems that there is little to be gained by further research into the characteristic of those who complete suicide in prisons. There is a relatively good understanding of this now. Indeed much of the recent research has begun to move on and to look at the best means of intervening to reduce suicide (e.g. Marzano, Hawton, Rivlin et al, 2016).

CHAPTER 9

Suicide in Prisons an Empirical Study of Prisoner Suicides from 1978 to 2014

Introduction

Earlier chapters have described and discussed previous research on completed suicides in prisons, primarily focusing on work in England and Wales. In this chapter a review of a more recent analysis of self-inflicted deaths is outlined. This work was undertaken for the Harris Review and was undertaken with assistance from analysts working in the UK Ministry of Justice (MoJ). The data reviewed below is largely descriptive and is based on the results summarised in the relevant statistical notice published by the MoJ as agreed with the research team partners (Ministry of Justice, 2015). This chapter provides a closer examination and exploration of the initial findings from this data.

Three pervasive themes can be seen to emerge from an examination of this data. Firstly, it raises the issue of how the data and findings sit in the context of previous empirical and qualitative research. In particular, the extent to which the findings provide confirmatory evidence of previous findings and the extent to which they suggest new and emerging trends in relation to prisoner suicide. Second, what new findings are there from the data? In addition to analysis of the data discussions with colleagues, in relation to the presentations at conferences at some of the initial findings, has been helpful in informing the thinking around this area. Third, there has been a dearth of theorising around prisoner suicide making it more difficult to build on and develop empirical findings. This neglected area of suicide in prisons is looked at in some detail, with a view to building a better theoretical understanding of suicidal behaviour in prisons and potentially across other settings.

The initial purpose of the analysis was to inform the work of the Harris Review. The review was described as a once in a life time opportunity to make a difference in reducing completed suicides (Harris, 2015). The review had a focus on those aged 18–24-years-old in prison custody. It rapidly became clear to the review team that, in order to do full justice to the 18–24-year-old group, there was a need to understand the data within the broader perspective of self-inflicted deaths across all age groups. Only by doing this would there be the capacity to have a meaningful benchmark to make comparisons with.

The data

The analysis included in the report published by the MoJ included a range of variables. These were based on what had been deemed interesting in previous research as well as what was accessible in the MoJ data set. This included: the rates of self inflicted deaths (SIDs) across different age groups, ethnicities, gender, sentence lengths, and offence types, the length of elapsed time in prison immediately prior to the SID, the method and location of the SID, and the proportion of SIDS where the prisoner had been formally classified as being identified as at an inflated risk of suicide at the time of their death. This latter classification was variously captured within the database. Administrative processes in connection with the management of the suicidal have changed a number of times over the years, resulting in changes to the way information was recorded. Currently the pertinent paperwork is called the Assessment, Care in Custody, and Teamwork (ACCT) documentation.

The data set is by no means perfectly accurate, with some data omissions such as, especially in the 1970s and 1980s, sentence length. However, overall the data set probably remains as one of the very best historically and internationally. There were 2,039 cases for the period of the research. The overall pattern was one of increased numbers and rates of self-inflicted deaths from 1978 to 2014. Although the prisoner population also increased markedly in size over this period, the rates of completed suicide increased, on average, faster. From 2002 onwards, when the rate was 133 per 100,000 (with the exception of small increase in 2007) the rates steadily decreased, with a relative low in deaths for 2011 of 68 per 100,000. This result may be argued to be both, on the one hand depressing, because the rates are still high, and on the other heartening. If the rates were to be reduced to the levels seen as recently as 2011 there would be a marked reduction in prisoner suicide at the time of writing, with deaths around half of those seen in 2016. This recent history also perhaps reflects the fact that there is a great deal of expertise amongst prison staff in reducing the risk of suicide but that this is not being used. One possible explanation of this is that there has, perhaps, been a reduced focus on this important area of work, in favour of other competing priorities.

Overall the data for 18–24-year-olds follows broadly the same pattern in terms of numbers of completed suicides as the overall prison population, although with sometimes a wider variance. This may plausibly be a statistical function of the smaller sample size for that group. Although the pattern in terms of rates was broadly the same, the substantive finding was that those in the 18–24-year-old age group have a relatively lower level of risk of completing suicide, when compared with the general prisoner population who will be on average older. However, the overall prisoner population is relatively young and as such, in terms of frequencies or actual numbers of suicides, these are more frequent amongst younger prisoners. This is a result of the overall age profile of the prison population, rather than an effect of age per se. But the consequence of this for 18–24-year-olds is that of a total of 706 self-inflicted deaths from 2004 to 2013, 133 of them were in the age group of 18–24 (six in children aged 15–17) but 205 in the age group 30–39. A total of 21 completed suicides were in the 60+ age category. The relative proportion and total number of older prisoners appear to be on the increase. If current trends were to continue unaddressed then it seems probable that future patterns based on the age profile and numbers of those imprisoned would continue. This suggests an increase in overall rates and numbers of completed suicides.

The highest number of completed suicides (from 2004 to 2013) was among 30–39-year-olds but the rate of completed suicides tends to increase with age, up to the age of 59. From the age of 60 onwards the rates begin to decrease. The key finding is that, on average, older prisoners are significantly more likely to complete suicide than younger prisoners. This is not a new finding but replicates several previous research findings. What is new is that the pattern is markedly different when the data is analysed through the lens of gender. The age pattern remains and is more marked for men, when women prisoners are removed from the analysis. Conversely when men are removed from the analysis the age pattern for completed suicides for women for the period of the study from 1978 to 2014 is reversed. In other words, younger women are, on average, at a higher risk of completing suicide than older women. There is at least one caveat to this finding, which is that this is based on a total number, which is about a twentieth the size of the number of men who have completed suicide over the period. Nonetheless this may well be a vital distinction in better informing policy and practices when working with suicidal prisoners.

In the literature and amongst commentators when rates of suicides are discussed they are sometimes conflated with the actual number of suicides. But even when this important distinction is made there is rarely a consideration of the patterns of the rates within age bands. For the data from 2002 to 2013 there have been different patterns for different age groups. For example, the rates amongst 18–39-year-olds generally declined during that period.

When looking at completed suicides and gender in the literature, a common problem has been that of the statistically small sample sizes for women and girls. Of course, in human terms, small numbers rather than large numbers is overwhelmingly positive. However, statistically (and otherwise) this makes the picking-out of meaningful patterns from the data more challenging. The number of women completing suicide peaked for the period of this research in 2003 with a total of 14 deaths. For the period of the research, overall increases in the number of suicides have been largely a reflection of growth in the number of men completing suicide. If age categories are looked at for women, for most years between 1978 and 1998 there were no recorded completed suicides, with a total of seven completed suicides over those 20 years. For the period from 2002 to 2013 the average rate of completed suicides was higher for women (at a rate of 117 per 100,000) than for men (at a rate of 92 per 100,000). As an illustration of the problem of small numbers when checking for rates if the high of one year, that is, 2003 is taken out of that analysis then the pattern is reversed in terms of overall rates for that period. For example, if the rates are calculated for the five years up to and including 2013 as they were in the research then the rate for men is 75 per 100,000 and 43 per 100,000 for women. Thus, there is a need to take a tentative approach when making any such general assertions in relation to the data on gender around self-inflicted deaths in prisons.

Notwithstanding the important caveat of statistically small numbers, as alluded to earlier in this chapter there do appear to be some discernible age differences in the patterns of completed suicides for women and men. Just as for men the pattern was that increased age came with an increased risk of completed suicide, the reverse was the case for women. But both these findings have interesting exceptions. With the data on women, the exception is girls (aged 15–17) who appear to be at a markedly lower level of risk than women aged 18 and over, based on rates of death. For men aged 60 and over the level of risk, based on rates, drops off in comparison with men aged in their 50s. Because of the small sample sizes although there is some coverage and speculation in relation to the various age band categories that the data is broken down into there is probably not much that can be sensibly understood further from such numerically very small sub-categories in terms of it as statistical data. That is not to say that much cannot be learnt from looking at the individual cases but this research was primarily quantitative in nature and lacks the potential richness of a qualitative design. These research findings were though influential in informing the Harris Review, in combination with findings derived from concurrent qualitative research, which was separately commissioned for the Harris Review.

Moving on from gender to ethnicity as a variable to consider one of the key findings of this research was, in keeping with research in the 1990s that suggested prisoners who self-identified as 'white' were significantly overrepresented in the figures both in terms of rates and numbers of completed suicides (Towl and Crighton, 1998). It is interesting that very little in the UK had been done prior to the 1990s to consider the impact of ethnicity on completed suicide rates. Indeed prior to 1989 ethnicity was not recorded on the safety in custody dataset in the Prison Service in England and Wales. Sometimes ethnicity had not been declared by the prisoner when going into prison and thus there was no data recorded in some cases in the completed suicide dataset. Although completed suicides generally increased for black prisoners and other minority ethnic groups from 1989 into the 21st-Century, the rate of increase was slower than for white prisoners.

International studies, and studies looking at prisons in England and Wales have previously indicated an underrepresentation of black prisoners when compared with white prisoners in the overall numbers and rates of completed suicides (Towl and Crighton, 1998). What has not been reported up until this research, is that the observed difference appears to have been growing, albeit with rates for both groups markedly increasing. In all years from 2004 to 2013, self-identified black prisoners had lower rates of completed suicide than white prisoners. However, although the pattern was broadly similar for Asian and mixed race categories, in 2008 the rate of completed suicides was greater for Asian than white prisoners and the same was so for mixed race prisoners in 2012. As with looking at gender there is a need to be mindful of the impacts of relatively small numbers on statistical analysis of these different categories. However, in terms of the fundamental findings it is evident that white prisoners remain over-represented in the completed suicide figures and that this appears to becoming more rather than less markedly so.

An area of previous research has involved analysis of the impacts of sentence length on likely risk of suicide. There are some interesting and novel findings here too with this research. Prisoners given determinate sentences of over ten years' imprisonment had even higher rates of completed suicide than those sentenced to indeterminate sentences. With this exception though sentence length in general was associated with an overall increase in the risk of completed suicide. Prisoners sentenced to between three and five years seem to have had some of the lowest rates of suicide from 2002 to 2013. So, what was replicated from past research was an inflated risk of suicide for indeterminate sentenced prisoners but the new findings here were twofold. First, the inflated risk for those with very long determinate sentences (over ten years) and second that there was no discernible overall link between sentence length and inflated risk of suicide.

Historically and internationally probably the most robust finding in the suicide in prisons literature has been the importance of the length of time which elapses once imprisoned. The first day in particular and also the first few weeks of imprisonment, have been generally viewed to be a time where there is a significantly inflated risk of suicide. This is one empirical reason why it makes little sense to administer screening instruments in that all will be at a markedly inflated risk of suicide on day one, for example.

Of those who completed suicide between 1978 and 2014 in prisons 24 per cent did so within a week of their arrival at the prison and 43 per cent did so within a month of their arrival. This pattern appears slightly amplified for those in the 18–24-year-old bracket that the Harris Review were particularly focused upon in terms of their remit (with figures of 26 per cent and 46 per cent respectively).

In general, the above finding was replicated in this research with a markedly increased risk of suicide during the early period of incarceration. However, one new finding is the discernible shift in the total percentage of completed suicides accounted for during the early period of imprisonment. So, between 2005 and March 2014 19 per cent of deaths occurred during the first week compared with 27 per cent from 1988 to 2004. This is a new and significant finding. This provides some evidence that the Prison Service focus, informed by the research, on the early period of imprisonment, has been effective to some degree in terms of early prevention.

Many prisoners who complete suicide are likely to be on remand. As a group remand prisoners, compared with sentenced prisoners, will tend to be earlier in their time in prison. Taking a snapshot of the population they will on average have spent less time in custody. Thus, it is most likely to be a function of time spent in prison rather than legal status which results in relatively high numbers of completed suicides by remand prisoners particularly early on during the period of imprisonment. There are fewer, and as their time in prison goes on, far fewer, remand prisoners that go on to complete suicide, relative to the sentenced prisoner population. Of course, there will be fewer prisoners held on remand for extended periods compared with sentenced prisoners.

Another variable included in the data analysis was offence type. Here, again, there were some findings that supported previous research but others that suggested new emerging trends in terms of the literature to date. Those convicted on violence against the person offences accounted for by far the largest number of total completed suicides, compared with any other offence category. This replicated consistent findings from previous research undertaken in this area both internationally and historically. This was followed, in terms of the actual number of such cases, with those held on remand or sentenced for sexual offences. The number of deaths in this group were though markedly lower than for violent offenders. Arson and criminal damage was the eighth most common offence type numerically. However, in terms of the rates of completed suicide, arson and criminal damage (with a rate of 142 per 100,000 population) showed higher rates than violence against the person prisoners (with a rate of 112 per 100,000) and sex offenders (with a rate of 108 per 100,000). Interestingly the offence type most commonly associated with completed suicide, for 18–24-year-olds, was sexual offences (with a rate of 96 per 100,000). Returning to the findings that have not been evident in the research previously, the over-representation by rate of completed suicide of those convicted of arson and criminal damage offences may have been missed, due to previous comparatively small sample sizes. This illustrates the importance of focusing on rates, as well as the absolute numbers, of completed suicides for sub-groups. Had there simply been a focus upon the total number of completed suicides then the inflated risk of this group by the measure of rate per 100,000 would not have been detected.

For the purposes of meeting the terms of reference from the Harris Review there was a focus on 18–20-year olds. A variable which had been a focus of some previous research was that of prison type. Such research went on to inform decisions around financial investment and a strategic approach to suicide prevention, which in the UK included targeting 'local prisons' . In the UK, the term 'local prison' refers primarily to those prisons which take remand and short sentence prisoners, directly from the courts. As such they tend to have a high turnover of population, with a relatively high proportion of acute problems associated with drug use and mental health. In these settings, there are consequent associations with an environment with an inflated risk of suicide for prisoners. There was though little difference between the level of inflation of risk by prison type for those in the 18-to-20-year-old groups.

There were unsurprising results when looking at the time of day, day of the week and month datasets for completed suicides. Between 12 midnight and 6 am accounted for around a third of completed suicides which is an over representation when compared with other six hour periods of the day. One of the difficulties with this data is the uncertainty around the timing and discovery of death with some variable recording practices. The peak time for recorded death appears to be between 5 am and 7 am, but it is unclear precisely when these deaths took place. The result may simply reflect the checking procedure times of night staff, before handing over to day staff. There were no differences by day of the week. This was broadly so for the different months too, albeit with a relatively small drop in February which may, to some degree, reflect that there are fewer days in February.

There has been much discussion and debate around the location within a prison of those who complete suicide. Nearly three quarters of completed suicides take place within what is referred to as a 'normal cell'. What is less clear, because of inadequate recording, is whether such cells have been shared or single. Although for some of the location categories there is clarity, for example, Segregation Units/Close Support Units which are highly suggestive of single cell accommodation. Less than one per cent of those who completed suicide did so in a 'safer cell'. This is an area which would benefit from better data, specifically it would be helpful to know how many safer cells there are in the Prison Service which could contribute to a better understanding of how safe or otherwise they are and what contribution they may best make to reducing the risk of prisoner suicide. A (high) level of completed suicides was evident from the data in prison healthcare centres. This raises interesting questions about how safe or otherwise healthcare centres are for the management of the suicidal. It may also simply reflect the most high risk cases being transferred disproportionately to healthcare centres within prisons. Similar arguments could be made about the relatively high levels of suicide in mental hospitals when compared with prisons. Very few completed suicides occurred outside the prison whilst under prison care but at a different location such as a hospital or court.

By far the most common method of suicide continued to be hanging. There were some gender differences. Around 90 per cent of men completed suicide by hanging compared to 80 per cent of women. Around nine per cent of women used self-strangulation, with relatively small numbers of overdoses for both women and men. Bedding was the main ligature material used followed by shoelaces which accounted for the method used with nearly 200 cases between 1978 and March 2014. In terms of ligature points, windows account for by far the most cases with over a 1,000 cases for the period of analysis in this research. Beds were used for ligature points in over 200 cases. Windows have become much less common as the ligature point since around 1999 to 2014 with light fittings becoming increasingly popular ligature points over that period. Nonetheless windows are still by far and away the most common ligature point used in accounting for completed suicides.

Another variable that was included for examination was that of the percentage and number of those who completed suicide who had been identified as at an inflated risk of suicide by staff. The documentation used to capture the case management of such prisoners was previously referred to as Form 2052 for Self-Harm or F2052SH procedures. These were introduced in 1995 and were subsequently revamped and launched (in 2007) as an Assessment, Care in Custody and Teamwork (ACCT) system, after a review through the now lamentably defunct Suicide Awareness Support Unit (SASU).

A higher percentage of women prisoners were identified through such procedures prior to their completed suicides. Interestingly, although broadly similar proportion of prisoners were subject to F2052SH processes as those of ACCT, this was not the case for 18–24-year-olds with a higher percentage being managed on the newer ACCT system. The proportion of those being managed using such administrative and case management systems was much the same irrespective of the ethnicity of the prisoners concerned. Probably the most striking feature when looking at the percentages of completed suicide cases who had been identified was that those over 60 were least likely to be managed under suicide prevention systems, with percentages at about half the average for those in the prison population overall who completed suicide.

There are several clear limitations of the data outlined above. It was not clear whether those in the 'not on an F2052SH or ACCT' category had ever been managed under these systems or not. Equally it was not evident how many prisoners had been managed through these systems successfully, insofar as they had not completed suicide. Around a quarter of all those completing suicides had been identified in advance as at an inflated risk of suicide. For many and probably most cases, as far as is currently known, those managed under ACCT and its predecessors did not go on to complete suicide. Most prisoners who complete suicide (around 75 per cent) are not identified in advance insofar as evidence of case management at the time of death is an accurate indicator of this. The gender based key finding is that at the time of death about a quarter of men were identified and about half of women were who went on to complete suicide. This may reflect different gender-based patterns of communicating distress and thus may make individuals more or less easy for staff to identify as in need of support, due to an increased risk of suicide. It may also reflect differences in culture between prisons. Alternatively, or additionally, it may simply be an artefact of statistically small numbers on the part of the women completing suicide.

The research also included an exploration of all deaths in prison whether self-inflicted or not. Although both deaths overall and self-inflicted deaths as a distinct category have increased over the period of study there remain some interesting patterns within the data set. For example, since 2008 the number of self-inflicted deaths was substantially lower than other deaths in custody not being suicide. This may, to some degree, reflect some of the changes in the prison population and environment. Unsurprisingly the percentage of classifications as 'natural causes' deaths increased with age, accounting for nearly all over 60 deaths and one in five of those between 15 and 17. Here it is evident that many prisoners arrive into custody with poorer health than the general population. This may in turn be linked to issues of substance use, as well as issues of poverty and poor access to healthcare in the community. In turn this may go some way to explaining the elevated rates of death because of natural causes.

An examination of deaths overall helps shed light on suicide in particular. It would be predicted that older prisoners would die more frequently per head than younger prisoners and this is indeed what is observed. Yet, as a cause of death, there is a greater probability that an older prisoner will complete suicide than a younger prisoner, despite there not being so many other causes of death in a prison environment that one might anticipate for a younger prisoner. This serves to highlight just how powerful the age effect is in relation to suicide particularly for older white men detained in prisons.

Despite having lower rates of completed suicide than older prisoners, young men aged between 18 and 24 accounted for 518 of the 2,014 such deaths between 1978 and 2013, which is around a quarter of all such deaths. This is a sobering reminder of the waste of these young lives. In 2003 and 2004 there were also a total of 27 completed suicides by women, 14 in 2003 and 13 in 2004. Between 1978 and 1988 there were a total of five cases of completed suicide by women. This illustrates how challenging it can be to discern meaningful patterns in the data given the overall statistically small numbers involved.

Theoretical Implications

There is a generally poor theoretical understanding of suicide in the mental health literature and explanatory models have been slow to develop (O'Connor and Nock, 2014). Linked to this, research progress has been slow and halting, in the absence of a means of integrating and directing empirical research. Historically research has often involved summaries of empirical data on self-inflicted deaths in the community. This critique is even more evident when specific populations, such as prisoners or children in custody are considered (Harris Review, 2015). Here there have been few attempts to develop theories that might inform and direct future research (Crighton, 2008).

In contrast, community-based studies have increasingly sought to integrate empirical findings with psychological models (O'Connor, 2011; Williams, Van der Does, Barnhofer et al, 2008). Such models have linked suicidal behaviour to fundamental research into human behaviour. In turn this has suggested a wide range of testable predictions that have illuminated the causal processes involved. These models have suggested a role for pre-existing vulnerability to suicide which may be the result of genetic factors as well as early adversity in childhood. Such vulnerability has often been referred to as 'diathesis' meaning a pre-existing vulnerability. For progression to suicide the role of adverse life events and stress reactions to these have been a focus. The responses that any person can make to difficulties are clearly dependent on what prior resources they can draw on, in combination with the scope to use these in each environment. Community-based research has identified many clear 'risk factors' for suicide, meaning factors that are associated with an increased risk of completing suicide. There has been less research into the area of 'protective factors', referring to factors that serve to reduce the risk of suicide but there is some emergent data in this area.

Research in prisons has, with some notable exceptions, lagged some way behind that in the community. This is despite the fact that prisons may provide a unique opportunity to better understand and reduce suicides, with wider implications for suicide research. Prisoners in general present with many risk factors for suicide. These include well known factors such as mental health problems. They will also frequently present with limited skills to manage difficulties in life (Liebling, 1991). In turn prisons, will serve to close off many ways of responding to stress and anxiety that prisoners may have relied on previously. Some of these responses may be dysfunctional, such as avoidance through for example substance use. Others may be functional but nevertheless will be less accessible, for example, access to family support.

Community-based research has noted associations between childhood adversities and later suicide. Such findings have been replicated in many studies which suggest a strong association of suicide with adverse events in childhood such as physical, sexual, and emotional abuse, family violence, parental illness, divorce and parental death. In turn this research has suggested a marked correlation between the severity and duration of such experiences and negative long term risk of suicide attempts. Here sexual and physical abuse during childhood appear to be the most predictive risk factors. As noted elsewhere in this text, prisoners as a group present with elevated levels of adverse childhood experiences of exactly this type.

In addition, there is a considerable body of research suggesting an association between feelings of hopelessness and the occurrence of suicide (Beck, Kovacs and Weissman, 1979). There is surprisingly little research into the effects of imprisonment and such feelings. Based on clinical experience though it seems reasonable to suggest that the experience of imprisonment is likely to generate increased feelings of hopelessness and helplessness. It may also exacerbate pre-existing vulnerability linked to such feelings. Researchers looking at the community have stressed the potential value in investigating the relative predictive usefulness of state versus trait hopelessness. Prisons seem to be an especially good setting to test such ideas and evaluate interventions to reduce such feelings as a means of reducing risk.

A classic study by Beck and colleagues reported that the vast majority of all suicides were associated with measures of impulsivity (Wenzel and Beck, 2008). This is an area that has been subject to extensive study over many decades. The association between suicide and impulsivity has not proved to be as clear or consistent as first thought. It is now felt that effects may be indirect (Gvion and Apter, 2011). Self-reported impulsivity has been associated with suicidal ideation, attempts and deaths. The meaning of impulsivity though has often been poorly defined and inconsistent, with some research focused on cognitive definitions and others on emotion-based definitions. This in turn has complicated interpretation of the role of impulsivity.

Issues of impulsivity appear to be similarly central to suicidal and related behaviours in prisons (Crighton, 2008; Crighton and Towl, 1997; Liebling, 1991; Towl and Crighton, 1998). Issues of impaired ability to control impulses is often a central area of need for prisoners. Many will present with poorer ability to control emotions and with limited cognitive skills to control impulses. This perhaps goes some way to explaining the past finding that educational courses in prisons that develop problem-solving skills, also reduced the risk of self-injury (Crighton, 2008). Links between poor impulse control and violence towards others also seem to be important in the context of prison suicides. Those who assault others, violently or sexually, show elevated rates of suicide. They will also frequently have difficulties with impulse control suggesting a link between violence towards themselves and others. Such links have been explored and theoretical models have been developed to test such associations (Plutchik, 1997).

Considering this it is suggested here that there are several important issues in taking forward research into suicide in prisons. First and foremost, there is a need to move beyond simple quantitative studies. Such research is likely to yield diminishing returns with few significant new insights into suicide in prisons. If work in this area is to progress, then it needs to link more closely to mainstream community-based research. There is also a need to link research in prisons to a clear theory base which produces a better understanding of the underlying psychological processes involved in suicide. In turn this may inform clinical and other interventions to reduce risk. Prisons seem to provide an ideal setting to develop a better understanding of suicide and how to reduce and prevent it. It is disappointing that in recent years this area of work in prisons has seen a reduction in focus and support for research and practice.

CHAPTER 10

Future Directions

Prisoners represent a selective sample of the general population. Social and legal processes result in many of the most disadvantaged ending up in prison custody. This includes higher rates of educational under achievement, poor mental health, homelessness and poverty being evident. With reductions in social and mental health care provision, prisons have often come to be, by default, a placement of last resort. In turn, prisons are not generally equipped to address the needs of an increasing population, with mounting health and social care needs. Many of those in prison custody should simply not be in such an environment as currently structured. In the context of suicide and indeed self-injury, the characteristics of the prison populations in the UK presents many challenges for prisons. Many of the risk factors for suicide and self-injury are evident in prison populations. As a result, prisons face an enormous challenge in addressing suicide.

This challenge is not new. The work of Smalley (1911) identified the risks of suicide in prisons in England and Wales and, in turn, built on work in the 19th-Century. More recent research such as that of Topp (1979) noted the upward trends in the rates of suicide in prisons, based on officially recorded suicide statistics. Looking at rates of suicide a progressive increase from 28 to 60 per 100,000 prisoners per year was observed. By current standards, such figures seem strikingly low. Looked at over the long term there has been a dramatic and sustained rise in the rates of suicide in prisons, with short periods where reductions were achieved. This is in the context of rates of suicide in the community reducing over several decades. Set in the social and historical context the current rates of suicide in prisons are both shocking and unacceptable.

The research into suicide in prisons has tended to confirm several consistent findings over time. It has also suggested several emerging changes. It has been consistently found that prisoners are at greatly increased risk of suicide compared to the general population It has also been evident that prisoners, as a group, do not closely resemble the general population in some key respects of relevance to the risk of suicide and other self-injurious behaviours. In the United Kingdom generally and England and Wales in particular, an increasingly large prison population is being drawn selectively from the general population. This large and growing population has arrived in prison with a variety of disadvantages. Those with mental health problems have increasingly found themselves in prison, often because of the absence of more appropriate mental health or social care provision. This means that direct comparisons between prisons and the rates of suicide in the general community are potentially misleading.

Post-millennial research into suicide in prisons has increasingly adopted public health approaches. This suggests a move away from sociologically-informed approaches that dominated in the 1980s and early-1990s. These sociological approaches had served an important and, many may argue critically important role, in stressing the need for broad-based approaches to suicide prevention, involving all those working in the 'prison community'. This moved suicide and self-injury away from a previous model which stressed solely healthcare assessment and prediction of suicide and self-injury, based on often inadequate and stretched primary care services in prison. It was accurately noted that primary care services alone could not reasonably be expected to manage these areas and that prevention and management needed to draw on a wider range of resources. In this respect the approach was entirely congruent with the public health approaches advocated (Plutchik, 1997).

There were initial gains from the implementation of these approaches. In prisons in England and Wales, this led to the establishment of the Suicide Awareness Support Unit (SASU), as a focus for implementation, research and development of suicide and self-injury prevention work (Towl, 2007). This increased emphasis led to a more targeted focus on reducing suicide in prisons and there were some associated reductions in suicides over a number of years that followed. There were though also limitations to the policy implementation. The reduced stress on health-care assessments may have led, in some prisons, to primary healthcare support being withdrawn or reduced to inadequate levels. This was often not matched by adequate training and support for prison officers to work effectively with suicidal prisoners: and more broadly with those experiencing mental health problems.

Two pervasive themes have dominated the area of suicide in prisons over at least the last century. Notions of human rights are often discussed in the context of the post-Second World War conventions in this area. They are though older than this and are central to the imprisonment of women and men. A central issue is that the state in taking away a person's freedom takes on a duty of care towards them. For prisoners, this is independent of what crimes they may have committed, or in the case of those imprisoned on remand have been accused of committing. In addition, there are issues surrounding the marked social and economic disadvantages of prisoners. Prisoners are often relatively poor with high rates of unemployment (both within and beyond the prison gates). Those from lower socio-economic groups have higher rates of suicide and unemployment is itself strongly associated with an increased risk of suicide. Added to these variables is the correlation between criminality and mental health problems. Those who are imprisoned by the courts have, on average, higher rates and numbers of mental health difficulties than the general population.

The prison environment is also central to any consideration of suicide. There is evidence to suggest that prison environments, with respect to suicide, are 'toxic' in the sense that they may increase risk. This effect may be even more marked for women than men in prison. Current notions of human rights stress the importance of the right to life and also the avoidance of inappropriate or unnecessary punishments. Such findings provide an argument that strengthens the case for far fewer women being imprisoned. Arguably this is something that needs to be weighed in policy terms and in court When sentenced to imprisonment the chances of a woman completing suicide is markedly increased, when compared with the increased level of risk for a man.

Earlier in this book, the context of imprisonment was introduced, followed by a wider discussion in relation to suicide. Theories of suicide as well as some of the community-based research in terms of the risk of suicide for the general population were covered. Also included earlier are aspects of the perspectives of various bodies such as the Ministerial Council, HM Chief Inspector of Prisons (and accompanying inspectorate) and Prisons and Probation Ombudsman. Some of the ideas and recommendations of the Harris Review and Howard League recommendations have also been touched upon. The later chapters of the book are intended as a key and concise resource summarising some of the key research on prisoner suicide to date. Uniquely this includes the largest international and historical study of suicide in prisons in England and Wales with over 2000 cases included in the review from 1978 to March 2014.

In this short and final chapter the focus is on what might be gleaned from the above, in terms of what is needed from a human rights perspective and with an evidence-informed focus. Potential improvements with an aim of a lowering of the numbers of completed suicides in prisons may be considered in terms of those where there would not be any additional financial resources needed and those where there would be. Also some changes involve broader system wide changes which although intended to have an impact in relation to suicide, this would be much broader than that. There are other changes, which could be made which may be viewed as suicide management specific.

There seems to be a growing consensus in the UK that current levels of imprisonment are too high and unsustainable, both socially and financially. This suggests a pressing need to reduce prisoner numbers in an appropriate way. This is a matter chiefly for Government and the courts. Within the UK, Government is responsible for making laws and policy. The role of the courts is to enact this through legal rulings and sentencing. Of course, the courts have some discretion in the way in which the laws are implemented in terms of some sentencing outcomes of their deliberations. Within the UK, there has been a sustained period of policy that has increased the length of prison sentences and increased the use of indeterminate imprisonment. Such measures clearly impact on the size of the prison population and also far more broadly. Any reversal of such policies will similarly have wider effects than reducing the number of suicides, which it would be expected to do.

Another general change, this time within the clear control of Ministers and HM Prison Service administration would be to radically change the Incentives and Earned Privileges (IEP) system. The IEP system reflects an application of simple behavioural reinforcement principles and would be generally seen as being a rather crude and simplistic approach. Modifications to reflect the importance of hope and the value of prisoner lives seem relatively easy to put in place quickly. In other terms, such behavioural systems do not need to be punitive, or perceived as punitive, particularly for the early periods of imprisonment. In fact, the adoption of punitive approaches is known to be generally ineffective and may result in marked adverse effects (Zimbardo, 2007). The use of punishments such as the prevention of visits from family and friends raises serious concerns in terms of suicide risk but also in terms of efforts to reduce risks to the wider community. All prisoners seem likely to benefit significantly from a right to more visits, particularly during the earlier stages of their imprisonment or following a move to a different prison. The controlled use of new technology to allow family communications also seems likely to be of great value, for example, allowing prisoners to send text messages to loved ones when they are moved to a different prison, with details of how to arrange a visit.

The measures outlined above would provide useful first steps to reducing suicide rates. They would also have several other advantages. Sending fewer women to prison would save money. It would also allow for the transfer of resources from prisons, which are largely ineffective for women, to community-based probation and social care services that may be more effective. Taking the Prison Service in England and Wales as an example, this could be simply done. A transfer of resources from very costly prison settings to the Probation Service, to ensure that there was sufficient support for community-based alternatives to custody provided via Probation Services, may give the courts more confidence in diverting more women from prison to viable and adequately resourced community sentences. Savings from such reorganization also goes beyond the individual prisoner, often impacting on their children and families, reducing the demands on social care, in the form of foster care or residential childcare. It can also be argued that reducing imprisonment may generate potential savings in the longer term, from possible lower rates of reoffending with community-based rather than prison-based interventions in view, in part, of their great ecological validity.

In recent years, there has been a limited political appetite to achieve such savings perhaps because of a concern about not being seen to be 'tough' on crime. Much of course hinges upon what being 'tough' looks like. Arguably, there are two elements, the traditional 'toughness' of punishment and hence sometimes harsh sentencing. Second a consideration of 'toughness' in terms of what is most effective in lowering the probability of future crimes. If both are considered in tandem, rather than tension, this may result in shorter sentences for some and longer community-based sentences for others. But this needs a high level of political will. It also requires a shift by prison administrators of resource from prisons to probation, representing a reversal of recent policies. The opportunity to do so may be the greater with the announcement of HM Prisons and Probation Service from April 2016.

Employment schemes for the unemployed would be one social policy that could impact in the long term on prisoner suicide rates. This could be achieved most directly by full employment in prisons. The current situation in prisons is one of chronic unemployment and underemployment. This represents a marked change of practice compared to the historic norms within prisons in the UK. Addressing the issue of chronic unemployment and underemployment in prisons has the potential to have a profound impact on overall suicide rates for prisoners. For those at elevated risk of suicide, long periods of social isolation, inactivity and boredom seem likely to have wholly deleterious effects. Recent years have seen a number of policy changes, aimed at addressing a range of skills gaps in the wider economy. This has included a growth in a wide variety of apprenticeship schemes designed to produce a more skilled workforce. Yet this area of social policy has had limited impact on prisons, which have remained largely isolated from such developments. Indeed, some jurisdictions have moved away from providing higher-level skills and educational training, in favour of low skill vocational courses such as industrial cleaning. The provision of high quality activities and training seem likely to reduce the risk of suicide for many in prisons and indeed for those on community-based sentences. The cost of financially supporting more work in prisons and apprenticeships would be likely to be less than current expenditure on many largely ineffective offending behaviour courses in prisons. Imprisonment clearly has a social role and will continue to do so. This does not though provide support for current practices in prisons in the UK in general and England and Wales in particular. Having chronically under-employed prisoners is bad for them and, in the longer term, bad for us all. Many could be trained through high quality apprenticeship schemes to suit their aptitudes, potentially increasing their employability and contributions to wider society. Arguably, prisons would benefit from more meaningful measures of their effectiveness. To take one example, prisons could benefit from a similar benchmark to that used in universities in the UK, which looks at the percentage of graduates in employment or further study six months after they have left. Such a measure of post-release employment for prisons would seem relatively simple to implement and to be more meaningful than internal measures of process and inputs.

Looking at the Prison Service for England and Wales, several untenable policy positions have been taken by prison administrators, in terms of prisoner suicide. Perhaps the most untenable of these is that, despite the dramatic rises in overall numbers of suicide, training for staff in this area is not currently mandatory. This sends a message about the way in which such training is viewed at a senior level. Equally, it is essential that staff need to have the confidence, knowledge and support to be able to deal with prisoners at risk of suicide. The current position whereby suicide prevention training has been downgraded to being non-mandatory will be seen to speak loudly about the priority given to the preservation of prisoner's lives. In human rights terms, this could not be more serious, given the centrality of the preservation of life. It can also be seen to reflect poorly on the Prison Service in England and Wales.

There is also a strong case for wider good quality staff training in mental health. Prisons have increasingly become the placement of last resort for those with mental health problems, as the provision of hospital and social care provision has reduced. Efforts to divert those with mental health problems from custody have largely failed in the absence of realistic alternative provision. Yet prison staff have not been equipped with the skills or support of specialist staff needed to work with these prisoners. This is clearly an area where there are costs attached and redeploying existing resources alone will not be likely to be sufficient in addressing it. Such training would be 'additional' to the current provision of training in prisons. It also suggests a need to recruit more allied health professionals to effectively help 'import' more generic health and social care expertise into the prison environment.

Another glaring need in relation to suicide in prisons is a simple administrative one, which has repeatedly been seen to afflict prisons. There is a straightforward need, in managerial terms, for appropriate record keeping. This is central to adequate communication and the effective management of suicide risk. Yet this is clearly not being achieved. The Harris Committee review, for example, noted that in prisons in England and Wales, Prison Service staff regularly failed to complete the ACCT documentation designed to manage suicide risks. The processes involved in this system, once a prisoner was identified as at high risk of suicide, were often not followed or, if they were, this was not recorded. It is difficult to see how there can be any convincing case as to why this has not been a management priority, or why it would not routinely be considered at senior management team meetings in prisons.

Distinct facilities for those prisoners aged over 50 could also be another development that may help in reducing prisoner suicide, with broader positive potential consequences too. The research in Europe is clear that the group most at risk in terms of suicide rates are those aged over 50. The needs of this group may well be different to that of younger prisoners. There may be intersectional effects in terms of the risk of suicide. So, for example, older sex offenders may be at an inflated risk of suicide with two flags of potentially inflated risk.

Life-sentenced prisoners are assessed more frequently than determinate sentenced prisoners for their risk of reconviction amongst other things. Such assessments by all concerned should routinely include a risk assessment of suicide. This is because, in terms of the evidence, it is well established that those with the most, in legal terms, serious offences are liable to have the highest risk of suicide. It also appears that the temporal pattern evident on average for the prisoner population, does not necessarily apply in the same way for those sentenced to life imprisonment. There is a need for a routine, but detailed, and particular, focus on support at critical points during such sentences. These would include the minimum tariff point set by the courts as well as other key points, such as Parole Board hearing, where details of the prisoners past and offence may be discussed in detail (at times in an adversarial manner) and significant such decisions may be made.

Women prisoners clearly have different needs to men. All too often though the default position in prisons has been for women and men to be treated in the same way. This might be framed in terms of equality of treatment but can be deeply unfair and inappropriate. It can be unfair because, for example, it may result in women being placed in custody further away from their homes, with family and visitors facing further to travel. There is also likely to be a greater probability that the children of women prisoners will go into state care if their mother is imprisoned. The nature of prison life for women can therefore be very different to that of men. Having access to visits and maintaining such contact can be an important element of suicide prevention. This suggests a need to place those women who need to be imprisoned in smaller units, closer to their home area, rather than the more administratively convenient approach of having a small number of larger women's prisons.

The culture in prisons is a significant issue and the research in this area has been informative. Prisons need to be well-managed to prevent the development of abuses (Towl, 2007; Zimbardo, 2007). Recent reviews (Harris, 2015) suggest there are hints of some of the problems of what some may have thought to have been confined to the past which may be re-emerging as the prison population has grown. For example, it is striking that HM Chief Inspector of Prisons (and inspectorate), responsible for inspecting prisons in England and Wales, still feel the need to emphasise the importance of something as basic as the need for staff to refer to prisoners in terms which are respectful. Prison managers at all levels perhaps need to be firmer in addressing inappropriate staff behaviours which may be other than suitably respectful. In turn, this provides a cultural context which it can be more difficult to evidence directly. It is though clear from previous reviews, commentaries and research that maintaining an appropriate culture in prison is essential, both in terms of prisoner safety but also in terms of prisons remaining humane and stable environments (Zimbardo, 2007).

In terms of clinical assessment of suicide risk the research and particularly the most recent research suggests a central role for such work. There has in the past been a reduction or stripping away of such support to staff in prisons. This seems at best ill-advised. The provision of adequate professional risk assessments, based on the current evidence-base, should have a central role in the management of suicidal prisoners. Past efforts to address this have often involved changes to the administrative systems surrounding suicide. Yet this has been largely ineffective where staff are untrained in such procedures and cannot access specialist and other resources to support them. Prisons in the UK appear to have generally suffered from this with changes in management systems such as ACCT in England and Wales and subsequent Prison Service Instructions being poorly matched to practice.

Above all though it can be convincing argued that there is now a need for urgent managerial action at the most senior levels. Further research, particularly where it is focussed on the scale of the problem, is likely to yield diminishing returns. There is a pressing need to free up the resources in prisons that are not productive. In turn, this would suggest a radical restructuring of services aimed at reducing suicide in prisons. In the UK, there are very strong arguments in favour of a change in focus and moving resources in a different direction to that seen, particularly in England and Wales, since 2005. In order to improve suicide prevention there is a need to focus at a policy level on reducing the prison population from current levels, in favour of community-based sentences and supervision. This is especially but not exclusively so for women. Such changes have the advantage of not being costly but involving better management of existing resources.

For those who need to be in prison there is a need for major cultural changes if suicide is to be reduced. At a fundamental level, prisons need to become positive and constructive environments. Chronically high levels of unemployment and under employment are likely to increase the risk of suicide, as well as having a range of other adverse effects. Similarly, environments where basic standards are not enforced seem likely to have damaging effects. The IEP scheme (above) needs to be terminated or radically changed. Psychological staff, for example, could readily be freed up from other priorities to focus upon saving the lives of prisoners. Prioritisation is just that.

For most prisoners being close to their home area is likely to have positive effects, making visits and social support more accessible. Yet for women and children detained in prison, this issue is likely to be more acute and there is a need for prisons to be designed around such needs for proximity, rather than administratively convenient large units.

Finally, there is a need to give priority to maintaining life by making training in this area fundamental to the role of prison staff. Training alone though is not sufficient and will be of limited value if staff cannot access specialist support and provision when needed, both in prison and in the community. There is also an urgent need to reverse the trend of reducing specialist resources in prisons that specifically address areas such as suicide and mental health needs. Ultimately, though, what is most important is not the administrative systems that are in place. Suicide prevention is above all, about people. It is about the values that people hold. It is fundamentally about the accepting and acting on the basis that prisoners' lives matter.

References

Adelstein, A. and White, G. (1976). Alcoholism and mortality. *Population Trends*, 6(7).

Ainsworth, M. D. S., Blehar, M. C., Waters, E. and Wall, S. (1978) *Patterns of Attachment: A psychological study of the strange situation.* Hillsdale, N J: Erlbaum.

Albanese, J. S. (1983) Preventing inmate suicides: A case study, *Federal Probation*, 47, 65–9.

Alessi, N. E., McManus, M., Brickman, A. and Grapentine, L. (1984). Suicidal behavior among serious juvenile offenders, *American Journal of Psychiatry*.

Amchin, J., Wettstein, R.M. and Roth, L.H. (1995) Suicide, ethics and the law. In S.J. Blumenthal and D. J. Kupfer (eds.) *Suicide Over the Life Cycle: Risk factors, assessment and treatment of suicidal patients.* Washington DC: American Psychiatric Association.

American Psychiatric Association (2015) *Diagnostic and Statistical Manual V.* Washington DC: American Psychiatric Association.

Appleby, L. (1992) Suicide in psychiatric patients: risk and prevention, *British Journal of Psychiatry*, 161, 749–58.

Appleby, L., Kapur, N., Shaw, J., Windfuhr, K., Williams, A., Hunt, I. M. and Ibrahim, S. (2015) *The National Confidential Inquiry Into Suicide and Homicide by People With Mental Illness Annual Report 2015: England, Northern Ireland, Scotland and Wales*, Manchester, University of Manchester.

Backett, S. (1987) Suicides in Scottish Prisons, *British Journal of Psychiatry*, 151, 218–21.

Barr, B., Taylor-Robinson, D., Scott-Samuel, A., McKee, M., and Stuckler, D. (2012) Suicides associated with the 2008–10 economic recession in England: time trend analysis, *British Medical Journal*, 345, e5142.

Barraclough, B. M., Bunch, J., Nelson, B. et al (1974) A hundred cases of suicide: clinical aspects, *British Journal of Psychiatry*, 170–102. Quoted in R. Jenkins, S. Griffiths and I. Wylie. (eds.), *The Prevention of Suicide*, Department of Health: London.

Barraclough, B. M. and Hughes, J. (1987) *Suicide: Clinical and epidemiological studies.* London: Croom Helm.

Battin, M. P. (1996) *The Death Debate: Ethical Issues in Suicide*, Upper Saddle River, NJ: Prentice Hall.

Beck, A. T. (1967) *Depression: Clinical, experimental and theoretical aspects*, New York: Harper Row.

Beck, A. T., Kovacs, M. and Weissman, A. S. (1979) Assessment of suicidal intention: the scale for suicidal ideation, *Journal of Consulting and Clinical Psychology*, 47, 343–50.

Board of Prison Commissioners (1911) *Annual Report*, London: Home Office.

Bogue, J. and Power, K. (1995) Suicide in Scottish prisons, 1976–93, *Journal of Forensic Psychiatry*, 6, 527–40.

Botsis, A. J., Soldatos, C. R. and Stefani, C. N. (1997) *Suicide: Biopsychosocial approaches*. Amsterdam: Elsevier.

Bridgwood, A. and Malbon, G. (1995) *Survey of the Physical Health of Prisoners, 1994: A Survey of Sentenced Male Prisoners in England and Wales, Carried Out by the Social Survey Division of OPCS on Behalf of the Prison Service Health Care Directorate.* London: HM Stationery Office.

British Psychological Society (2011) *British Psychological Society Statement on the Open Letter to the DSM-5 Taskforce.* Leicester: British Psychological Society.

Brockington, I. F., Kendell, R. E. and Leff, J. P. (1978) Definitions of schizophrenia: Concordance and prediction of outcome, *Psychological Medicine*, 8, 387–98.

Brown, G. W. and Harris, T. O. (1978) *Social Origins of Depression*, London: Tavistock.

Brown, G. W. and Harris, T. O. (1993) Aetiology of anxiety and depressive disorders in an inner city population. 1 Early adversity, *Psychological Medicine*, 16, 739–44.

Brown, G. W. and Prudo, R. (1981). Psychiatric disorder in a rural and an urban population: 1. Aetiology of depression, *Psychological Medicine*, 11(03), 581–599.

Bulusu, L. and Alderson, M. (1984) *Suicides 1950–82. Population Trends*, 35, 11–17. HMSO: London.

Chappell, C. A. (2004) Post-secondary correctional education and recidivism: A meta-analysis of research conducted 1990–1999, *Journal of Correctional Education*, 55(2), 148–169.

Charlton, J. (1995) Trends and patterns in suicide in England and Wales, *International Journal of Epidemiology*, 24, s45-s52.

Charlton, J., Kelly, S., Dunnell, K., Evans, B. Jenkins, R. and Wallis, R. (1992) Suicide deaths in England and Wales: trends in factors associated with suicide deaths. Reprinted in R. Jenkins., S. Griffiths., I. Wylie (eds.), The Prevention of Suicide, Department of Health: London.

Charlton, J., Kelly, S., Dunnell, K., Evans, B. and Jenkins, R. (1992) Suicide deaths in England and Wales: Trends in factors associated with suicide deaths. Reprinted in R. Jenkins., S. Griffiths., I. Wylie (eds.) *The Prevention of Suicide*. Department of Health: London.

Cherlin, A. J., Furstenberg, F. F., Chase-Lonsdale, P. et al (1991) Longitudinal studies of effects of divorce on children in Great Britain and the United States, *Science*, 252, 1386–89.

Chesney, E., Goodwin, G. M. and Fazel, S. (2014) Risks of all-cause and suicide mortality in mental disorders: a meta-review, *World Psychiatry*, 13(2), 153–160.

Coid, J., Wilkins, J., Coid, B. and Everitt, B. (1992) Self-mutilation in female remanded prisoners II: A cluster analytic approach towards identification of a behavioural syndrome, *Criminal Behaviour and Mental Health*, 2, 1–14.

Crewe, B. (2012) *The Prisoner Society: Power, adaptation and social life in an English prison*, Oxford: Oxford University Press.

Crow, T. J. (1995.) The two syndrome concept: origins and current status, *Schizophrenia Bulletin*, 16(3), pp. 433–443.

Crittenden, P. M. and Claussen, A. H. (eds.) (2003) *The Organization of Attachment Relationships: Maturation, culture and context*, New York: Cambridge University Press.

Crighton, D. (1997) The psychology of suicide, *Issues in Criminological and Legal Psychology*, 28, 36–44.

Crighton, D. A. (2006) *Approaches to Reducing Reoffending in Custody and the Community*, Review Paper Office of the Chief Psychologist, London: Home Office and Department of Health.

Crighton, D. A. (2008) *Reducing Reoffending Follow up Review*, Review Paper, Office of the Chief Psychologist, London: Ministry of Justice.

Crighton, D. A. and Towl, G. J. (1997) *Self-Inflicted Deaths in England and Wales 1988–1990, and 1994–95*, In G.J. Towl (ed.) *Suicide and Self-Injury in Prisons, Issues in Criminological and Legal Psychology*, 28, British Psychological Society: Leicester.

Crighton, D. A. and Towl, G. J. (2002) Intentional self Injury. In G. Towl, M. McHugh and L. Snow (eds.), *Suicide in Prisons*, Leicester: British Psychological Society.

Crittenden, P. *Danger, Development and Adaption: Seminal Papers on the Dynamic-Maturational Model of Attachment and Adaptation* (2015), Landini A., Hart M., Baim C. and Landa S (eds.), Sherfield-on-Loddon: Waterside Press.

Crombie, I. K. (1989) Trends in suicide and unemployment in Scotland 1979–86, *British Medical Journal*, 298, 782–784.

Crombie, I. K. (1990) Can changes in the unemployment rates explain the recent changes in suicide rates in developed countries, *International Journal of Epidemiology*, 19, 412–416.

Crow, T. J. (1980) Molecular pathology of schizophrenia: More than one disease process? *British Medical Journal*, 280 (6207), 66–68.

Cullen, J. E. (1985) Prediction and treatment of self-injury by female young offenders, in Farrington, D. P. and Tarling, R. (eds.), *Prediction in Criminology*, Albany, NY: State University of New York Press.

Curran, L., McHugh, M. and Nooney, K. (1989) HIV counselling in prisons, *Counselling Psychology Quarterly*, 2(1), 33–51.

Cutler, J., Bailey, J.E. and Dexter, P. (1997) Suicide awareness training for prison staff: an evaluation. In G.J. Towl. (ed) *Suicide and Self-Injury in Prisons, Issues in Criminological and Legal Psychology*, 28, British Psychological Society: Leicester.

Dexter, P. M. and Towl, G. J. (1994) An investigation into suicidal behaviour in prison, in N. K. Clark and G. Stephenson (eds), Criminal behaviour: perceptions, attributions and rationalities, *Issues in Criminological and Legal Psychology*, 22. British Psychological Society: Leicester.

Diekstra, R. F. W. and Hawton, K. (eds.) (1987) *Suicide in Adolescence*, Dordrecht, NL: Martinus Nijhoff Publishers.

Dooley, E. (1990a) Prison suicide in England and Wales, 1972–87, *British Journal of Psychiatry*, 156, 40–45.

Dooley, E. (1990b) Unnatural deaths in prison, *British Journal of Criminology*, 30(2), 229–234.

Durkheim, E. (1952) *Suicide*, London: Routledge and Kegan Paul.

Fairburn, G. (1995) *Contemplating Suicide: The language and ethics of self-harm*, London: Routledge.

Farrington, D. P. (1993) *The Challenge of Teenage Anti-Social Behaviour*, Paper prepared for the Martach Castle Conference on 'Youth in the Year 2000'.

Farrington, D. P. (1994) Childhood, adolescent, and adult features of violent males, in L. Rowell Huesmann (ed.) *Aggressive Behaviour: Current perspectives*, Boston, MA: Springer.

Farrington, D. P. (1995) The development of offending and antisocial behaviour from childhood: Key findings from the Cambridge Study in Delinquent Development. *Journal of Child Psychology and Psychiatry*, 6(36), 929–964.

Farrington, D. P. (2015a) The developmental evidence base: Prevention. In D. A. Crighton and G. J. Towl (eds.), *Forensic Psychology* (2nd edition), Chichester: John Wiley and Sons.

Farrington, D. P. (2015b) The Developmental evidence base: Psychosocial research, in D.A. Crighton and G.J. Towl (eds.), *Forensic Psychology* (2nd edition), Chichester: John Wiley and Sons.

Farrington, D. P., Loeber, R. and Van Kammen, W. B. (1990) Long-term criminal outcomes of hyperactivity-impulsivity, attention deficit and conduct problems in childhood, in L. N. Robins and M. Rutter (eds.) *Straight and Devious Pathways From Childhood to Adulthood,* Cambridge: Cambridge University Press.

Fazel, S., Bains, P., and Doll, H. (2006) Substance abuse and dependence in prisoners: A systematic review, *Addiction*, 101(2), 181–191.

Fergusson, D. M., McLeod, G. F., and Horwood, L. J. (2013) Childhood sexual abuse and adult developmental outcomes: Findings from a 30-year longitudinal study in New Zealand, *Child Abuse and Neglect*, 37(9), 664–674.

Ferguson, C. J. (2013) Spanking, corporal punishment and negative long-term outcomes: A meta-analytic review of longitudinal studies, *Clinical Psychology Review*, 33(1), 196–208.

Fonagy, P., Steele, M., Steele, H., Higgitt, A. and Target, M. (1994) The theory and practice of resilience, *Journal of Child Psychology and Psychiatry,* 35(2), 231–57.

Forrester, A., Exworthy, T., Olumoroti, O., Sessay, M., Parrott, J., Spencer, S. J. and Whyte, S. (2013) Variations in prison mental health services in England and Wales, *International Journal of Law and Psychiatry*, 36(3), 326–332.

Fox, H. A. and Shewry, N. (1988) New longitudinal insights into relationships between unemployment and mortality, *Stress and Health,* 4(1), 11–19.

Freiberg, K., Homel, R., and Lamb, C. (2013) The pervasive impact of poverty on children: Tackling family adversity and promoting child development through the pathways to prevention project, *Pathways and Crime Prevention*, 226.

Fulton, R. (2008) *Review of the Forum for Preventing Deaths in Custody,* Ministry of Justice.

Harlow, H. F., and Harlow, M. K. (1965) The affectional systems, *Behavior of Nonhuman Primates*, 2, 287–334.

Goring, C. (1913) *The English Convict,* Darling: London. Quoted in Topp, D.O. (1979) Suicide in prison, *British Journal of Psychiatry*, 134, 24–7.

Gvion, Y. and Apter, A. (2011). Aggression, impulsivity, and suicide behavior: A review of the literature, *Archives of Suicide Research*, 15(2).

Hawton, K., Linsell, L., Adeniji, T., Sariaslan, A. and Fazel, S. (2014) Self harm in prisons in England and Wales: An epidemiological study of prevalence, risk factors, clustering and subsequent suicide, *The Lancet*, Vol. 383, March, 29, London.

The Harris Review (2015) *Changing Prisons, Saving Lives, Report of the Independent Review into Self inflicted Deaths in Custody of 18–24-year-olds*, July, London: OCL.

Hatty, S. E. and Walker, J. R. (1986) *A National Study of Deaths in Australian Prisons.* Canberra: Australian Centre of Criminology.

Hawton, K. (1994) Causes and Opportunities for prevention, In R. Jenkins, S. Griffiths and I.Wylie (Eds.), *The Prevention of Suicide*, London: HMSO.

Hawton, K., Comabella, C. C., Haw, C. and Saunders, K. (2013) Risk factors for suicide in individuals with depression: A systematic review, *Journal of Affective Disorders*, 147(1), 17–28.

Hawton, K., Saunders, K. E. and O'Connor, R. C. (2012) Self-harm and suicide in adolescents, *The Lancet*, 379(9834), 2373–2382.

Hawton, K. and Fagg, J. (1992) Trends in deliberate self-poisoning and self-injury in Oxford, 1976–90, *British Medical Journal*, 304, 1409–11.

Hawton, K., Fagg, J., Simkin, S. et al (1997) Trends in deliberate self-harm in Oxford, 1985–19995, *British Journal of Psychiatry*, 171, 556–60.

Hawton, K., Comabella, C. C., Haw, C. and Saunders, K. (2013) Risk factors for suicide in individuals with depression: A systematic review. *Journal of Affective Disorders*, 147(1), 17–28.

Hawton, K., Saunders, K. E., and O'Connor, R. C. (2012) Self-harm and suicide in adolescents, *The Lancet*, 379(9834), 2373–2382.

Haycock, J. (1989) Race and suicide in jails and prisons, *Journal of the National Medical Association*, 81, 405–11.

Herbert, K., Plugge, E., Foster, C. and Doll, H. (2012) Prevalence of risk factors for non-communicable diseases in prison populations worldwide: A systematic review, *The Lancet*, 379(9830), 1975–1982.

Hetherington, E. M. (1989) Coping with family transitions: winners, losers, and survivors, *Child Development,* 60, 1–14.

Hetherington, E. M., Cox, M. and Cox, R. (1982) Effects of divorce on parents and children, in M. Lamb (ed.) *Nontraditional Families,* Hillsdale, NJ: Erlbaum.

HM Government (2016) *Commons Select Committee Report on Prison Safety,* London.

HM Inspector of Prisons for England and Wales (1990) *Review of Suicide and Self-harm.* London: Home Office

HM Inspector of Prisons for England and Wales (1999) *Suicide is Everyone's Concern: A thematic review,* London: The Stationary Office.

HMI of Prisons (2012) *Expectations: Criteria for assessing the treatment of prisoners and conditions in prisons,* Version 4, London: HMI.

HMI of Prisons (2014) *Expectations; Criteria for assessing the treatment of prisoners and conditions for women in prisons,* Version 1, London: HMI.

Howard League for Penal Reform and Centre for Mental Health (2016*) Preventing Prisoner Suicide, Perspectives from the inside,* London: Centre for Mental Health.

Home Office (2003) *Driving Delivery: A strategic framework for psychological services in prisons and probation,* London: HM Prison Service and National Probation Service.

Horowiz, A.V. and Schied, T. L. (eds.) (1999) *A Handbook for the Study of Mental Health: Social contexts, theories and systems,* New York: Cambridge University Press.

Humber, N., Webb, R., Piper, M., Appleby, L. and Shaw, J. (2013) A national case–control study of risk factors among prisoners in England and Wales, *Social Psychiatry and Psychiatric Epidemiology,* 48(7), 1177–1185.

Independent Advisory Panel on Deaths in Custody (2015) *Deaths in Custody: An examination of the cases 2000 to 2014,* Independent Advisory Panel on Deaths in Custody, London: IAP.

Independent Advisory Panel on Deaths in Custody (2017) *Deaths in State Custody: Statistical Release 2015,* London: IAP

ICD (1993) *The ICD-10 Classification of Mental and Behaviourial disorders, Clinical Descriptons and Diagnostic Guidelines,* WHO.

Ivanoff, A. and Jong, S. J. (1991) The role of hopelessness and social desirability in predicting suicidal behaviour: A study of prison inmates, *Journal of Consulting and Clinical Psychology,* 59, 394–99.

Jablensky, E. (1981) quoted in Kendell, R. E. (1994) Mood (affective) disorders in R. E. Kendell and A. K. Zealey (eds.) Companion to Psychiatric Studies (5th edn.) Edinburgh: Churchill Livingstone.

Jenkins, R., Bhugra, D., Bebbington, P., Brugha, T., Farrell, M., Coid, J. and Meltzer, H. (2008) Debt, income and mental disorder in the general population, *Psychological Medicine*, 38(10), 1485–1493.

Joiner, T. E. (2005) *Why People Die By Suicide*, Boston, MA: Harvard University Press.

Jones, A. (1986) Self-mutilation in prison: a comparison of mutilators and non-mutilators, *Criminal Justice and Behaviour*, 13, 286–96.

Jones, N. L. (1996) An Empirical Study of Suicidal Behaviour in Prisons, Unpublished M.Sc. Dissertation, University of London.

Kazminan, L. and Farrington, D. P. (2015) The developmental evidence base: Desistance, in D. A. Crighton and G.J. Towl (eds.), Forensic Psychology (2nd edn.) Chichester: John Wiley & Sons

Kelly, S. and Bunting, J. (1998) Trends in suicide in England and Wales, 1982–1996, *Population Trends*, 92, 29–41.

Kim, R. H. and Clark, D. (2013) The effect of prison-based college education programs on recidivism: Propensity score matching approach, *Journal of Criminal Justice*, 41(3), 196–204.

Kinderman, P. (2015) Beyond disorder. In D. A. Crighton and G. J. Towl, G. J. (eds.) *Forensic Psychology*, Chichester: John Wiley & Sons.

Klerman, G. L. and Weissman, M. M. (1989) Increasing rates of depression, *Journal of the American Medical Association*, 261, 2229–35.

Kerkhof, J. F. M. and Bernasco, W. (1990) Suicidal behaviour in jails and prisons in The Netherlands: Incidence, characteristics and prevention, *Suicide and Life Threatening Behaviour*, 20, 123–37.

Kirk, S. A., Cohen, D., and Gomory, T. (2015) DSM-5: The delayed demise of descriptive diagnosis, in *The DSM-5 in Perspective* (63–81), The Netherlands: Springer.

Kreitman, N. (1977) (ed.) *Parasuicide*, London: Wiley & Sons.

Lang, W. A., Ramsey, R. E., Tanney, B. L. and Tierney, R. J. (1989) Caregiver attitudes in suicide prevention, in Diekstra, R. F. W. et al (eds.), *Suicide and Its Prevention*, Leiden: E. J. Brill.

Lester, D. (1991) Physical abuse and physical punishment as precursors of suicidal behaviour, *Stress Medicine*, 7, 255–6. Quoted in Livingstone, M. (1997).

Liebling, A, (1991) Suicide in Prisons, Unpublished PhD Thesis. University of Cambridge.

Lin, N., Dean, A. and Ensel, W. M. (eds.) (2013) *Social Support, Life Events, and Depression,* Amsterdam: Academic Press.

Lingham, R. (1995) Mental Health and Risk Management. Symposium presented at the Institute for the Study of Delinquency annual conference, University of Nottingham.

Liu, J. and Raine, A. (2006) The effect of childhood malnutrition on externalising behavior, *Current Opinion in Pediatrics,* 18(5), 565–570.

Livingstone, M. (1994) Self-injurious behaviour in prisoners. Unpublished Ph.D. thesis, University of Leeds.

Livingstone, M. (1997) A review of the literature on self-injurious behaviour amongst prisoners, in G.J. Towl. (ed.) *Suicide and Self-Injury in Prisons, Issues in Criminological and Legal Psychology,* 28, Leicester: British Psychological Society.

MacCormick, A. H. (1931) *The Education of Adult Prisoners: A Survey and a Program,* New York: National Society of Penal Information.

MacDonald, M. (2013) Women prisoners, mental health, violence and abuse. *International Journal of Law and Psychiatry,* 36(3), 293–303.

MacAskill, S., Parkes, T., Brooks, O., Graham, L., McAuley, A. and Brown, A. (2011) Assessment of alcohol problems using AUDIT in a prison setting: more than an 'aye or no' question, *BMC Public Health,* 11(1), 1.

Maccoby, E. E. (1998) *The Two Sexes: Growing up apart, coming together,* Cambridge, MA: Belknap Press.

MacLeod, A.K., Williams, J.M.G. and Linehan, M.M. (1992) New developments in the understanding and treatment of suicidal behaviour, *Behavioural Psychotherapy,* 20(3), 193–218.

Malinosky-Rummell, R., and Hansen, D. J. (1993) Long-term consequences of childhood physical abuse, *Psychological Bulletin,* 114(1), 68.

Marshall, T., Simpson, S. and Stevens, A. (2000*) Healthcare in Prisons: A health care needs assessment,* Birmingham: University of Birmingham.

Marzano, L., Hawton, K., Rivlin, A., Smith, E. N., Piper, M. and Fazel, S. (2016) Prevention of suicidal behavior in prisons, *Crisis.*

McHugh, M. J. and Towl, G. J. (1997) Organizational Reactions and Reflections on Suicide and Self-Injury in G. J. Towl (ed.) *Suicide and Self-injury in Prisons, Issues in Criminological and Legal Psychology,* 28 Leicester: British Psychological Society.

Mechanic, D. (1999) Mental health and mental illness: definitions and perspectives, in A. V. Horowitz and T. L. Schcid (eds.) *A Handbook for the Study of Mental Health: Social contexts, theories and systems,* New York: Cambridge University Press.

Menninger, K. A. (1938) *Man Against Himself,* New York: Harcourt Brace.

Mental Health Act 1983

Ministry of Justice (2015) *Statistical Notice, Self Inflicted Deaths in Prison Custody in England and Wales between 1978 and March, 2014,* London: Ministry of Justice.

Ministry of Justice (2015) *Government Response to the Harris Review into Self-inflicted Deaths in National Offender Management Service Custody of 18–24-year-olds,* London, Ministry of Justice.

Ministry of Justice (2015) *Statistical Notice: Self-Inflicted Deaths in Prison Custody in England and Wales between 1978 and March 2014,* London: Ministry of Justice.

Mok, P. L., Kapur, N., Windfuhr, K., Leyland, A. H., Appleby, L., Platt, S. and Webb, R. T. (2012) Trends in national suicide rates for Scotland and for England and Wales, 1960–2008, *British Journal of Psychiatry,* 200(3), 245–251.

Morgan, H. (1979) *Death Wishes? The understanding and management of deliberate self-harm,* New York: John Wiley & Sons.

Moser, K. A., Fox, A. J. and Jones, D. R. (1984) Unemployment and mortality in the OPCS longitudinal study, *Lancet* ii: 1324–8.

Moser, K. A., Goldblatt, P., Fox, A.J. and Jones, D.R. (1990), in Goldblatt, P. (ed.) *Longitudinal study 1971–81: Mortality and social organisation,* OPCS LS series. London: HMSO.

Neeleman, J., Mak, V., and Wessely, S. (1997) Suicide by age, ethnic group, coroners' verdicts and country of birth. A three-year survey in inner London, *British Journal of Psychiatry,* 171(5), 463–467.

Nicholson, J. M., Fergusson, D. M. and Horwood, L. J. (1999) Effects on later adjustment of living in a stepfamily during childhood and adolescence, *Journal of Child PsychoMinisterial Council on Deaths in Custodylogy and Psychiatry,* 40(3), 405–416.

Nisbett, R. and Ross, L. (1980) *Human Inference: Strategies and shortcomings of social judgement.* Engelwood Cliffs, NJ: W. H. Freeman.

National Offender Management Service (2011), *Prison Service Instruction 64/2011 (Safer Custody),* London: NOMS.

O'Carrol, P. W. (1993) Suicide causation: Pies, paths and pointless polemics, *Suicide and Life Threatening Behaviour,* 12, 27–36.

O'Connor, R.C. (2011) Towards an integrated motivational–volitional model of suicidal behaviour in R. C. O'Connor, S. Platt and J. Gordon (eds.), *International Handbook of Suicide Prevention: Research, policy and practice*, Chichester: John Wiley & Sons.

O'Mahoney, P. (1990) Prison suicide rates: what do they mean? Paper presented at the Deaths in Custody conference, Canterbury.

Obafunwa, J. O. and Busuttil, A., (1994) A review of completed suicides in the Lothian and Borders region, *Social Psychiatry and Psychiatric Epidemiology*, 29, 100–106.

Oltmanns, T. F. and Maher, B. A. (eds.) (1988) *Delusional Beliefs*, New York: Wiley.

Parsloe, P. (1976) Social work and the justice model, *British Journal of Social Work*, 6(1), 71–89.

Patterson, G. R., Forgatch, M. S., Yoerger, K. L. and Stoolmiller, M. (1998) Variables that initiate and maintain an early-onset trajectory for juvenile offending. *Development and Psychopathology*, 10(03), 531–547.

Pattinson, E. M. and Kahan, J. (1983) The deliberate self-harm syndrome, *American Journal of Psychiatry*, 140, 867–72.

Paykel, E. S. and Cooper, Z. (1992) Life events and social stress, in E. S. Paykel (ed.) *Handbook of Affective Disorders*, Edinburgh: Churchill Livingstone.

Platt, S., Backett, S. and Kreitman, N. (1988) Social constructions or causal ascription: distinguishing suicide from undetermined deaths, *Social Psychiatry and Psychiatric Epidemiology*, 23, 217–22. Quoted in R. Jenkins, S. Griffiths, I. Wylie, K.Hawton, G.Morgan and A.Tylee (1994) (eds.) *The Prevention of Suicide*, London: Department of Health.

Platt, S. and Kreitman, N. (1984) Unemployment and parasuicide in Edinburgh 1968–82, *British Medical Journal*, 289, 1029–32.

Plous, S. (1993) *The Psychology of Judgement and Decision-making*, New York: McGraw Hill.

Plutchik, R. (1980) *Emotion: A psychoevolutionary synthesis*, New York: Harper Row.

Plutchik, R. (1993) Emotions and their vicissitudes: Emotions and psychopathology, in M. Lewis and I. M. Havilland (eds.) *Handbook of Emotions*. New York: Guilford.

Plutchik, R. (1994) *The Psychology and Biology of Emotions*, New York: Harper Collins.

Plutchik, R. (1997) Suicide and violence: The two stage model of countervailing forces, in A. J. Botsis, C. R. Soldatos and C. N. Stefanis (eds.) *Suicide: Biopsychosocial approaches*, Amsterdam: Elsevier.

Plutchik, R. and Van Praag, H. M. (1990) A self-report measure of violence risk, II, *Comprehensive Psychiatry*, 31, 450–56.

Plutchik, R., Van Praag, H. M., Comte, H. R. and Picard, S. (1989) Correlates of suicide and violence risk I: The suicide risk measure. *Comprehensive Psychiatry*, 30, 1–7.

Pokorny, A. D. (1983) Prediction of suicide in psychiatric patients, *Archives of General Psychiatry*, 40, 249–257.

Prisons and Probation Ombudsman (2014) *Learning from PPO Investigations, Self Inflicted Deaths of Prisoners on ACCT*, London: PPO.

Prisons and Probation Ombudsman (2015) *Self-Inflicted Deaths of Prisoners—2013/14*, London: PPO.

Prisons and Probation Ombudsman (2015) *Learning from PPO investigations: Risk factors in self-inflicted deaths*, London: PPO.

Rivlin, A., Hawton, K., Marzano, L. and Fazel, S. (2010). Psychiatric disorders in male prisoners who made near-lethal suicide attempts: case-control study, *British Journal of Psychiatry*, 197(4), 313–319.

Rossau, C. D. and Mortensen, P. B. (1997) Risk factors for suicide in patients with schizophrenia: nested case-control study. *British Journal of Psychiatry*, 171, 355–59.

Rothman, K. J. and Greenland, S. (eds.) (1998) in *Modern Epidemiology* (2nd edn) Philadelphia, PA: Lippincott Raven.

Rutter, M., Tizard, J., Yule, W., Graham, P. and Whitmore, K. (1976) Isle of Wight studies, 1964–1974, *Psychological Medicine,* 6(02), 313–332.

Rutter, M. and Taylor, E. A., (eds.) (2005) *Child and Adolescent Psychiatry*, Oxford: Blackwell.

Ryff, C. D. (1989) Happiness is everything or is it? Explorations of the meaning of psychological well-being, *Journal of Personality and Social Psychology*, 57, 1069–1081.

Sandstrom, M. J., and Coie, J. D. (1999) A developmental perspective on peer rejection: Mechanisms of stability and change, *Child Development*, 70(4), 955–966.

Schmidtke, A., Bille-Braher, U., DeLeo, D. et al(1996) Attempted suicide in Europe: rates, trends and sociodemographic characteristics of suicide attempters during the period 1989–1992. Results of the WHO/EURO multicentre study on parasuicide, *Acta Psychiatrica Scandinavi*a, 93, 327–38.

Schneidman, E. (1985) *Definition of Suicide*, New York John Wiley & Sons:

Shneidman, E. S. (1987) A psychological approach to suicide in G. R. Vanden Bos and B. K. Bryant (eds.) *Cataclysms, Crises and Catastrophes: Psychology in action.* Washington, DC: American Psychological Association.

Schotte, D. E. and Clum, G. A. (1987) Problem-solving skills in suicidal psychiatric patients, *Journal of Consulting Clinical Psychology*, 55, 49–54.

Shaw, J., Baker, D., Hunt, I. M., Moloney, A. and Appleby, L. (2004) Suicide by prisoners, *British Journal of Psychiatry*, 184(3), 263–267.

Shea, S. J. (1993) Personality characteristics of self-mutilating male prisoners, *Journal of Clinical Psychology*, 49, 576–85.

Sheiban. B. K. (1993) Mental illness and suicide in Israel, *Medical Law*, 12, 445–65, Quoted in Plutchik (1997).

Skeels, H. M. and Dye, H. B. (1939) A study of the effects of differential stimulation on mentally retarded children. Proceedings and Addresses, American Association for Mental Defectiveness, 44, 114–115.

Skodal, A. E. and Karasu, T. K. (1978) Emergency psychiatry and the assaultive patient, *American Journal of Psychiatry*, 145, 202–205.

Sletten, I. W., Everson, R. C. and Brown, M. L. (1973) Some results from an automated state wide comparison among attempted, committed, and non-suicidal patients, *Suicide and Life Threatening Behaviour*, 3, 191–7. Quoted in A. J Botsis et al (eds.) (1997).

Smalley, H. (1911) *Report by the Medical Inspector*. Report by the Prison Commissioners. London: Home Office.

Smith, P. K., Cowie, H. and Blades, M. (2004) *Understanding Children's Development*, Oxford: Blackwell.

Snow, L. (1997) A pilot study of self-injury amongst women prisoners, in G. J. Towl (1997) (ed.), *Suicide and Self-Injury in Prisons, Issues in criminological and legal psychology*, 28, Leicester: British Psychological Society.

Social Exclusion Unit (2002) *Reducing Reoffending by Ex-prisoners*, London: Cabinet Office.

Suicide Act 1961.

Thomas, A. and Chess, S. (1996) *Temperament: Theory and Practice (Basic principles into practice)* New York: Brunner Mazel.

Topp, D. O. (1979) Suicide in prison, *British Journal of Psychiatry*, 134, 24–7.

Towl, G. J. (1996) Homicide and Suicide, Risk Assessment in Prisons, *The Psychologist*, September, Leicester: British Psychological Society.

Towl, G. J. (1997) (ed.) *Suicide and Self-Injury in Prisons, Issues in Criminological and Legal Psychology*, 28, Leicester: British Psychological Society.

Towl, G. J. (2015) Concluding themes: Psychological perspectives and futures, in D. A. Crighton and G. J. Towl (eds.), *Forensic Psychology* (2nd edn.) Chichester: John Wiley & Sons.

Towl, G. J. (ed.) (2006) *Psychological Research in Prisons*, Oxford: BPS Blackwell.

Towl, G. J. and Crighton, D. A. (1996), *The Handbook of Psychology for Forensic Practitioners*, London: Routledge.

Towl, G. J. and Crighton, D. A. (1997) Risk assessment with offenders, *International Review of Psychiatry*, 9, 187–93.

Towl, G. J. and Crighton, D. A. (1998) Suicide in prisons in England and Wales from 1988 to 1995, *Criminal Behaviour and Mental Health*, 8, 184–92.

Towl, G. J. and Fleming, C. (1997) Self-inflicted deaths of women prisoners, *Forensic Update*, 51, 5–8.

Towl, G. J, Snow, L. and McHugh, M. J, (eds.) (2000) *Suicide in Prisons*, Oxford: BPS Blackwell.

Towl, G. and Walker, T. (2015) Prisoner Suicide, *The Psychologist*, 28, 886–889.

Towl, G. and Crighton, D. (2016) The emperor's new clothes?, *Psychologist*, 29(3), 188–191.

Towl, G. J. and Hudson, D. I. (1997) Risk Assessment and Management, in Towl, G. J. (ed). *Suicide and Self-Injury in Prisons, Issues in Criminological and Legal Psychology*, 28, Leicester: British Psychological Society.

Van Os, J., Castle, D. J., Takei, N., Der, G. and Murray, R. M. (1996) Psychotic illness in ethnic minorities: Clarification from the 1991 census, *Psychological Medicine*, 26(01), 203–208.

VanEgmond, D. and Diekstra, R. F. W. (1989) The predictability of suicidal behaviour, in Diekstra, R. F. W. et al (ed.), *Suicide and Its Prevention*, Leiden, NL: E. J. Brill.

Vaughan, B., Egeland, B., Sroufe, L. A and Waters, E. (1979) Individual differences in infant-mother attachment at 12 and 18 months: Stability and change in families under stress, *Child Development*, 50, 971–75.

Walker T. and Towl G. J. *Preventing Self-injury and Suicide in Women's Prisons* (2016), Sherfield-on-Loddon: Waterside Press.

Walsh, B. W. and Rosen, P. M. (1988) *Self-mutilation: Theory, Research and Treatment*, New York, Guilford Press.

Watts, F. N., Powell, E. G. and Austin, S. V. (1973) The modification of abnormal beliefs, *British Journal of Medical Psychology*, 46, 356–63.

Wenzel, A. and Beck, A. T. (2008) A cognitive model of suicidal behavior: Theory and treatment, *Applied and Preventive Psychology*, 12, 189–201.

Wilkinson, R. (1996) *Unhealthy Societies, The Afflictions of Inequality*, London: Routledge.

Williams, K., Poyser, J. and Hopkins, K. (2012) Accommodation, homelessness and reoffending of prisoners: Results from the Surveying Prisoner Crime Reduction (SPCR) survey, *Ministry of Justice Research Summary*, 3, 12, London: Ministry of Justice.

Williams, J. M. G., Van der Does, A. J. W., Barnhofer. T., Crane, C. and Segal, Z. S. (2008) Cognitive reactivity, suicidal ideation and future fluency: Preliminary investigation of a differential activation theory of hopelessness/suicidality, *Cognitive Therapy and Research*, 32, 83–104.

Williams, J. M. G. and Scott, J. (1988) Autobiographical memory in depression, *Psychological Medicine*, 18, 689–95.

Williams, K., Poyser, J. and Hopkins, K. (2012) Accommodation, homelessness and reoffending of prisoners: Results from the Surveying Prisoner Crime Reduction (SPCR) survey, *Research Summary*, 3, 12.

Wilson, E. O. (1980) *Sociobiology*, Cambridge, MA: Belknap Press.

Wilson, E. O. (2000) *Sociobiology, The new synthesis*, Havard University Press.

Wilson, M. (1993) DSM III and the transformation of American psychiatry, *American Journal of Psychiatry*, 150, 399–410.

Winkler, G. E. (1992) Assessing and responding to suicidal jail inmates. *Community Mental Health Journal*, 28, 317–326.

Wool, R. J. and Dooley, E. (1987) A study of attempted suicides in prison inmates, *Medicine, Science and the Law*, 27, 297–301.

World Health Organization (1993) *International Classification of Diseases* (10th revision) Geneva: World Health Organization.

Wright, J., Binney, V. and Smith, P. K. (1995) Security of attachment in 8–12-year-olds: A revised version of the Separation Anxiety Test, its psychometric properties and clinical interpretation, *Journal of Child Psychology and Psychiatry*, 36, 757–74.

Zimbardo, P. G. (2007) *Lucifer Effect*, New York: Random House.

Index

Preventing Self-injury and Suicide in Women's Prisons
Tammi Walker and Graham Towl
Foreword Lord Toby Harris

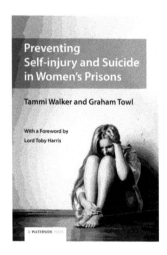

In 2015 the landmark suicide of the 100th woman to kill herself in prison custody passed largely unnoticed. This book by two experts sets out to redress the balance by examining all aspects of the history, present practices, causes and prevention prospects connected to this tragic chain of events. A long overdue analysis of a subject that is at last beginning to receive enhanced scrutiny. Focuses on both women and adolescent girls in custody. Looks at psychological, demographic, environmental and clinical factors. The first book of its kind.

'Great coverage of the key issues… really helpful tips on supporting women, on staff training and on managing the aftermath of a suicide. I highly recommend this book'
Professor Rory O'Connor, University of Glasgow.

'Very helpful in identifying the strengths and weaknesses of current practice and understanding why reductions in the prison population and a holistic approach to care are vital in saving lives'
Dr Jo Borrill, University of Westminster.

Paperback | ISBN 978-1-909976-29-0 | 2016 | 184 pages

Transgender Behind Prison Walls
Sarah Jane Baker
Foreword Pam Stockwell

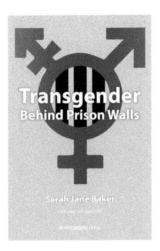

This first book on transgender in a prison setting looks at the entire HM Prison Service regime for such people. Ranging from hard information about rules and regulations, the transition process and how to access it to practical suggestions about clothing, wigs and hairpieces, make-up and coming out, the book also deals with such matters as change of name, gender identity clinics, hormones, medication and use of prison showers and toilets.

'An important contribution to current debates on the treatment of transgender prisoners'
Mia Harris, Oxford University.

'I was heartbroken. It felt like a bereavement. The young man I had come to love as a son had disappeared overnight, and been replaced by a girl who was not my daughter, but, I felt, a stranger'
Pam Stockwell (From the Foreword).

Paperback | ISBN 978-1-909976-45-0 | 2017 | 160 pages

Lightning Source UK Ltd.
Milton Keynes UK
UKHW020609130220
358664UK00006B/556